Beyond the Bleep

the definitive unauthorized guide to
What The Bleep Do We Know?!

Alexandra Bruce

disinformation®

Published by:
The Disinformation Company Ltd.
163 Third Avenue, Suite 108
New York, NY 10003
Tel.: +1.212.691.1605
Fax: +1.212.691.1606
www.disinfo.com

Library of Congress Control Number: 2005928851

ISBN-13: 978-1-932857-22-1
ISBN-10: 1-932857-22-2

Cover design: Jacob Rosette, Maya Shmuter, and Christina Piluso
Text design & layout: Maya Shmuter

Printed in USA
10 9 8 7 6 5 4 3

Distributed in USA and Canada by:
Consortium Book Sales and Distribution
1045 Westgate Drive, Suite 90
St Paul, MN 55114
Toll Free: +1.800.283.3572
Local: +1.651.221.9035
Fax: +1.651.221.0124
www.cbsd.com

For Tamara Kahan Bruce

MEDIA BUZZ FOR
WHAT THE BLEEP DO WE KNOW!?

"There's a bit of marketing genius behind the low-budget indie movie, **What the Bleep Do We Know?** Because: You see the movie. You come out dying to talk about it with friends, but you can't unless they've seen it, so you urge them to go. They repeat the process: seeing, dying, urging…Bleeping brilliant."
– KIM ODE
Minneapolis Star Tribune

"The most bizarrely intriguing movie I've seen in a long while…I couldn't turn it off. In fact, as soon as I finished watching it the first time, I immediately started up the DVD screener again to give it a second go…**What the Bleep Do We Know?** is a film about quantum physics, spirituality — and the meaning of life…It's full of head-scratchers, and the kind of talk I'm not used to hearing from scientists and other academics. The ambitious film attempts to answer existential conundrums such as: What is God? What are emotions? What is the soul? And the ever-popular why are we here?"
– CATHLEEN FALSANI
Chicago Sun-Times

"The independent film **What the #$*! Do We Know?** asks such weighty questions as 'What is reality?' and 'Who am I?'…To which some people in Hollywood have added a third query: How did this little film, out of nowhere and ignored by the big studios, sell $7.4 million in tickets?"
– JOHN LIPPMAN
The Wall Street Journal

"A film that is often dazzling. The best parts of this movie are the interconnecting collage of interviews with physicists, doctors, theologians, a molecular engineer and the 35,000-year-old warrior named Ramtha...They discuss with wit, wisdom and passion the possibilities encountered when one starts asking questions such as, 'Who are we?,' 'Why are we here?,' 'What divides and connects mind and brain, body and soul?,' 'What is the nature of love?' and 'What is real?' It's reminiscent of the late-night dorm room discussions, but instead of a bunch of bleary-eyed undergraduates, the participants are people who have devoted their lives to such questions...A deeply spiritual work that takes for granted that most people are hungry to break out of the sleep-walking existence of our consumer culture...Another reason it seems so different and has stirred such powerful reactions among viewers: This is a film that dares to treat people as smart and deeply curious rather than dumb and deeply cynical."
– TOM MAURSTAD
The Dallas Morning News

"Makes a strong case that quantum physics will impact our future in ways that are now almost unimaginable...puts a positive spin on the jolt to the intuition that is quantum physics, and suggests that a man's fate could be an enlightened new paradigm...The sum of all this is very powerful."
– WILLIAM ARNOLD
Seattle Post-Intelligencer

"**What the #$*! Do We Know?** A small film that mixes quantum physics, animation and documentary filmmaking is spreading across the country like a New Age fad diet."
– SCOTT BOWLES
USA TODAY

"It had its world premiere in the little town of Yelm, WA. (pop 3,289). It's an odd hybrid of science documentary and spiritual revelation, featuring a Greek chorus of Ph.D.s and mystics talking about quantum physics…Yet this idiosyncratic indie film has become a sleeper hit…The explanations of physics are so visual — and yes, understandable — that even moviegoers who struggled with high school math are enthralled."
– DAN CRAY
Time Magazine

"Mind-bending."
– KEVIN CRUST
Los Angeles Times

"**What the Bleep?!** has developed into a word-of-mouth hit following a gradual nationwide rollout that began nine months ago in a small Washington town. As it's opened in more and more theaters, it's garnered repeat business from many moviegoers. Some have even formed discussion groups to talk about the film's attempt to create a unified theory of reality by combining ideas from quantum physics, neural science, and mystical philosophy…But the movie's longevity in theaters…may reflect a

growing interest among some segments of American society in the connections between mind, body, and spirituality."
– STEPHEN HUMPHRIES
The Christian Science Monitor

"What the #$*! Do We Know?! is a movie that attempts to explain quantum physics in terms anyone can understand. It succeeds, up to a point...charming, intelligent, articulate and by definition baffled."
– ROGER EBERT

ACKNOWLEDGEMENTS

I am most grateful to Gary Baddeley for giving me the chance to do the impossible and for letting me say whatever I wanted!

Special thanks to my secret physicist advisor and to Disinformation's Ralph Bernardo, whose math skills helped us to avert grave embarrassment.

Most of all, I would like to thank the producers of the film phenomenon, *What The Bleep Do We Know!?* and to express my gratitude to each one of the outstanding people who were interviewed in the film. Their hard work and hard thinking are an inspiration to millions of people around the world.

Publisher's Note: This book is a direct result of my father, John Baddeley, emailing me about *What The Bleep Do We Know!?* long before it reached New York, let alone his village in the United Kingdom. (The amazing viral power of the Internet!) I hope you like it Doon.

Beyond the Bleep

TABLE OF CONTENTS

Contents

Beyond the Bleep

FOREWORD

This little book aims to be a helpful "Cliff Notes" on some of the competing cutting edge quantum physics and neuroscience ideas featured in the film *What The Bleep Do We Know!?* The most recent published works of the scientists interviewed in the film are summarized for those who want to know more about these fascinating subjects but who may not have the time or money to read them all.

What The Bleep Do We Know!? is the first commercial feature film to take on such complicated topics as theoretical physics, neurochemistry and trance channeling. The constraints of the cinematic format are such that these subjects could only be touched upon. Similarly, this book only digests the works of the extraordinary people profiled in the film. Those whose curiosity is piqued by what they find here are strongly urged to read the authors' books in their entirety. Over the course of studying their writings, I have been very moved by the life work and the achievements of the people interviewed in *What The Bleep Do We Know!?*

There has been controversy around some scientific claims made in the movie and especially around the entity known as Ramtha. This book aims to advise the reader about these controversies in the most even-handed and unbiased manner possible. At the time of this writing, I have no affiliation with the filmmakers or with the people portrayed in the film. This book also hopes to shed some light on the social forces at work behind the film's production and on the stark divergence of responses it has received.

– Alexandra Bruce

CHAPTER 1
THE *WHAT THE BLEEP* PHENOMENON

"Nobody in their right mind would have financed this movie."

Will Arntz
Financier and Co-Director of *What The Bleep Do We Know?!*

Like it or not, it is nothing short of astounding that this film got made at all. That a novice triumvirate of Hollywood outsiders got it made, got it seen and have made a handy profit without a distribution deal — after getting ripped to shreds by some critics — is a complete miracle. As if depicting the mind-bogglingly complex subjects of quantum physics, neuroscience and spirituality in a low budget feature length film was not enough of a challenge! Yet, within the strictures of its cinematic format, **What The Bleep Do We Know?!** succeeds impressively in presenting many of these ideas.

Not everyone agrees with me. Many reviewers found it easier to be contemptuous and disparaging rather than to take the film's intriguing ideas into consideration. Ignorant critics trashed the scientists interviewed in the film, apparently having no time to research who and what they were writing about before spewing something nasty in time for their deadlines. For example, Candace Pert, Ph.D., who is a Research Professor of Physiology and Biophysics at Georgetown University Medical School, the author of successful books on these subjects, who triggered a revolution in neuroscience while still in her mid-20s and who may yet be the person who discovers the cure for AIDS, is identified as "someone's completely random grandma wearing a tie-dye," who is "treated on screen as [an expert]."[1]

THE CULTURAL DIVIDES

Public reaction to *What The Bleep Do We Know!?* has revealed some interesting divisions in America, of which we may not have been previously aware. Where the second Bush presidency had already fueled the cultural rift between religious and non-religious communities, the reaction to the film has exposed a significant divide within the non-religious sector; namely that between the atheists and the spiritualists. It has also underscored a disconnect between secularist Hollywood and two potentially lucrative markets that are not being served: the religious and the spiritualist. And as we have seen, possible generational issues have been exposed, where Gen X and Generation Y viewers may have been bummed out by flashbacks of their acid casualty elders, in the Ur-Boomer stylings of some of the interviewees.

This was bound to happen in a film that endeavors to scientifically explain spirit and to spiritualize science. The science press, which is mostly atheist, has ravaged the film because it does not welcome the association of science with spirituality (and especially science with Ramtha), this despite the fact that most of the science discussed in the movie is mainstream. Religious people are understandably offended by the film's potshots at organized religion, in addition to disagreeing with the mysticism the film promotes. However, secular spiritual seekers, who welcome the aid of modern science to help them to understand their inner lives are overjoyed to buy multiple copies of the DVD to give to their friends and family:

[*What The Bleep*] served to bring into relief the need for constructive dialogue about the relationship among religion, philosophy, and science. When these diverse fields intersect today, the debate that follows is often stunted and acrimonious. Those with spiritual concerns claim that science extends beyond its rightful bounds and in effect disenchants the world. For their part, many scientists are reluctant to explore the philosophical implications of their work and content to ignore any metaphysical questions that might arise from it.[2]

There must be something unusual going on when many people are buying multiple copies of the film at the same time as divergent groups are saying things like the following about it:

> **Columbia University mathematics professor:** …it was certainly the stupidest thing I can remember seeing in a movie theater, and that's saying quite a lot (I see a lot of movies…). The whole thing is really moronic beyond belief.[3]

> **Christian viewer in Minnesota:** Our beliefs are called "backwoods" and "ugly." We are made fun of for believing that God could be so personal that He cares whether we sin or not. For, according to them, not only is the "real" god so great that he doesn't care about us piddley mortals, "how can you sin against a god so great as he who creates all this" but there is no such thing as "good" and "bad." Let's not even go that route….

If I can convince at least two Christians NOT to see this movie, I will feel like the sixteen dollars we gave those people to make fun of our beliefs will cancel itself out. Please let me know by response if you won't see this movie, I feel like I was duped! I wish I had had all this information before I went to see a movie I thought was about SCIENCE.[4]

THE SILENT MAJORITY?

Who are the takers of this film, who are neither the Ivy League university mathematician nor the Middle American Christian, cited above? In an interview in the *San Francisco Chronicle*, physicist Fred Alan Wolf, who appears in the film, offered his views:

> **Wolf:** When the film opened in Portland [OR], I was there to answer questions from the audience, and I could tell that these were the type of people who are the true silent majority in this country. America today isn't in the religious Right — even though there are millions of people in that movement. It isn't in the antireligious Left, either. It's in the center, and I think those are the people who caught on to the film…the spiritual experience is really what people hunger for, and I think the film addressed that hunger. People came away from it with that exaltation or excitement that comes when you have a spiritual awakening. Movies can sometimes provide that kind of opening in people, and this one did that.[5]

"The center" can be anybody…

> **Arntz:** Yeah, preaching to the choir is great and everything, but the huge payoff with the film is the people in the mainstream. We used to tell everyone

to tell all their friends they think would be into the film to go see it. And then we stopped saying that. Now we say, Tell everyone because you can never tell who's going to respond.

Interviewer: Any unexpected fans?

Arntz: A friend was in a Gold's Gym in L.A. and he was walking by a couple of really big weightlifter guys there — you know, with muscles on top of muscles. They were talking about the film and how great it was. My friend just kind of stopped and thought, "Holy Moses, I would never have thought these big beef-packers would be interested in this film." But there's a lot of people my friend calls metaphysical lost souls. People who, once they get exposed to this information, immediately get it. And they go with it. But this stuff's never been presented in a way like we're doing — accessible and kind of fun — and it doesn't have the dogma. It's safe. It's not like attending an encounter group where everyone is going to turn and stare at you and say, "What do you think?" It's a movie.

Co-Director Mark Vicente offers this view:

Vicente: People are so tired of living this old reality they've been fed. They're tired of trying all these things that haven't worked. And when they think about their problems, they feel helpless and don't think they have the power to change. What this film does is say: There is a science and there are ideas that are so wonderful that suggest that we have enormous power locked within us. What we're suggesting is that you have divinity inside you, that it's leaking out all the time and you have the power to change. People love that idea. It's much more interesting than thinking you're just a mindless speck on the face of the planet that has no say, and that there's a god outside of you keeping score and you have to supplicate yourself in front of that god before you get what you want. That's a stupid idea. This other idea — that maybe you are that god — is far more enticing.[6]

Because Hollywood has striven to avoid boycotts from any religious group, it has tended to shy away from religious or spiritual themes. No major distributor would touch Mel Gibson's *Passion of the Christ*, despite his formidable track record at the box office. This has turned out to be much to the distributors' chagrin, since according to the *Hollywood Reporter*, *Passion* "has the potential to wind up as the biggest grossing film in movie history."[7]

Similarly, Will Arntz was unable to find a distributor to finance **What The Bleep Do We Know?!** and, like Gibson, he was compelled to dig into his own pockets to produce his movie. But unlike Gibson, Arntz did not already have a well-financed production company like Icon to front the marketing costs of *Passion*. Arntz's team, therefore, devised novel strategies to release their film in theaters:

> **Arntz:** We know that Hollywood is a copycat town. Once they realize there's a vast market for this kind of cinema, it's going to get really interesting. And one of our intents is to basically have what Steven Simon [the producer of *What Dreams May Come*] is always championing: a spiritual cinema. Every week you can go to a movie theater and there are two or three movies that are talking to this audience.[8]

THE GUERRILLA MARKETING

Most independent feature-length motion pictures are never theatrically released but instead, after a possible stop or two at film festivals, go "straight to video," to generate income in the lucrative home video market (one actor friend of mine likes to point out that many films only go "straight to poster"!). Arntz and his collaborators were not satisfied with the idea of their film only playing on the small screen, so they made agreements with individual owners of movie theaters:

> **Arntz:** We started the film off last February in a little town called Yelm, WA, where a couple of us were living at the time. We pleaded with the local theater, on our knees, and said, "Look, we know enough people in town. We can sell it out for a couple of weeks." First they said no, no, no — but then they said, "OK, kids, we'll give you a week, but don't count on it." And we ended up having a seven-week run there. Then the Baghdad Theater in Portland, OR, where they'd been saying no to us all along, started saying, Oh, these box-office numbers are kind of interesting. Then they said, "OK, we'll give you a week, but you have to have 1,600 people show up. Otherwise we're going to pull it — and don't hold your breath, kid, we're probably going to have to pull it." So instead of getting 1,600 the first week, we got 4,500. And every week it went up 500 until, at its peak, about 7,000 people a week were seeing this film. It ended up playing there for 18 weeks.[9]

Using their grassroots web-based coordination of "Street Teams," they were able to generate business and then replicate the success they achieved on their home turf in other spiritualist-friendly regions, such as Sedona, Arizona, certain communities in Northern and Southern California, Hawaii, etc. Below is their strategy, as posted on the *What The Bleep* website. Now that the US theatrical run has ended, "Street Teams" are being drafted for international markets:

1. You sign up to your prospective country below.
2. You will be contacted by a Street Team Coordinator to get the ball rolling.
3. You will help us learn more about the area you live in and share what radio stations, clubs, groups, and organizations you think we should contact.
4. As a Street Team member we will provide you with promotional items from our Street Teams kit.
5. You will stay in touch with our Street Team Coordinator via e-mail or phone on how well it's going and include the e-mail addresses of anyone interested in street teaming, or in being on our mailing list.
6. You will be greatly blessed, and you will be joyful in the knowledge that you are uplifting the consciousness of the planet![10]

Their tactic of region-based self-marketing for a niche audience proved so successful, that they finally landed a distribution deal with independent, but respectable, theatrical distributors Samuel Goldwyn/Roadside Attractions, who released the film on 60 screens five months after the filmmakers' original release. Perhaps more significantly, the very mainstream and powerful Fox Home Video, part of Rupert Murdoch's News Corp. empire, picked up home video rights and has marketed the DVD very aggressively. The DVD sales pattern so far has been vigorous, if unusual:

A Fox spokeswoman says 11% of the online consumer pre-orders for Bleep at Foxstore.com have been for multiple copies. That's far more than the 3% for *The Passion of the Christ*, which was considered unusually high.[11]

THE QUANTUM CRUISE

In a possible backlash against the growing theocratic trend in American government, a brisk little business is building up around this "little film that could" — this book, included.

The *What The Bleep* website's Calendar page[12] shows that all of the scientists interviewed can be booked for speaking engagements directly through the film's website. They are apparently being kept quite busy, supplementing their teachers' salaries with speaking fees. Fred Alan Wolf and Masaru Emoto currently appear to be the most popular acts, with Amit Goswami, William Tiller and Candace Pert filling up the ranks behind them.

The seven Axiom *What The Bleep Prophet's Conferences* scheduled for 2005 alone should gross at least $1.3 million by my reckoning, not including merchandise and hotel revenue. This also does not count the many other conferences and speaking engagements and even a couple of Caribbean Cruises that have been lined up, one of which is billed as "The Quantum Cruise."[13]

Lest there be those who chafe at all of this shameless spiritual profiteering, they might ask themselves how they feel about TV programming that exploits bloodlust — or the $14 billion US pornography business — or the ultra fat coffers of countless Evangelists, such as Pat Robertson, Jerry Falwell, or Tim LaHaye, who does a bang-up business selling the apocalyptic "Rapture" to his flock — or how they feel about capitalism, itself.

Even if making money is the primary motivation behind the proponents of *What The Bleep*, it is hardly immoral for them to make a living promoting the ideas and people they admire. Is it such a bad thing that lectures on quantum physics and neuroscience are no longer restricted to college students and can now be had aboard a cruise ship? There is evidently a market for such things, albeit a different market from the one that subscribes to "The 700 Club."

> It is a parallel world created by an American system where caste and self-identity are determined by what one consumes, or cannot afford to consume, education and of course, the class into which one is born. Like most things American, it was about money from the get-go.[14]

CHAPTER 2
HOW DOES REALITY WORK?

The success of **What The Bleep Do We Know?!** points to a growing number of people looking for a deeper understanding of reality and of their own lives through models inspired by quantum mechanics. The existential implications of quantum physics have hit the streets, with a promise to bridge the gap between science and faith, between knowledge and mystery.

Though its initial equations have been around for a hundred years and despite its practical applications in thousands of everyday products, from computers to cell phones, quantum mechanics has somehow managed to evade popular recognition. True, the advanced math and mystifying jargon associated with physical theory have done little to help spread quantum physics awareness. The title of the syndicated television series "Quantum Leap" — a show which had little to do with quantum anything — did not help either. The proliferation in the 1980s and 1990s of the word "Quantum" as a futuristic-sounding brand name for incongruent products, ranging from vitamins to fishing tackle, has also unwittingly upheld the inherent imponderableness of this subject.

This chapter endeavors to explain, in the simplest terms, the quantum theories invoked by the scientists interviewed in **What The Bleep Do We Know?!** and to address some of the problems encountered in the film's presentation of these ideas. We will also challenge some of the scathing reviews the film has received on the alleged grounds of junk science and/or New Age fatuousness.

WARNING!

First, the reader needs to be warned that the deeper one delves into the subject of quantum physics, the more intimidating it becomes — but do NOT be intimidated! If you do not understand something on the first reading, do NOT shut down! It may take several readings of some passages in order for the ideas to sink in — but they WILL sink in and the insights into reality that they convey will titillate you!

Most people reach a point with quantum physics where they have gone as far "down the rabbit hole" as they need to go. I sure have! Those who never stop are the quantum physicists. To these people, the endeavor and the knowledge are everything. They are an interesting and fabulous breed! It has been an incredible experience to digest the works of the amazing people in this film and I encourage anyone reading this to do the same.

Because these ideas are extremely specialized, arcane and the subjects of contentious argument and controversy and I am not a physicist myself, I enlisted the help of a prominent European quantum physicist to analyze several of this book's passages. Since the theoretical physics community is very small and competitive, my advisor preferred to remain anonymous. He responded to my questions by email as well as by posting them on his two blogs, which I invite readers to check out: http://www. opensys.blogspot and http://www.opensys.blogsome

WHAT IS QUANTUM PHYSICS?

Quantum physics is a set of theories that are described by

mathematical equations, which explain and predict events that occur at atomic and subatomic levels. The subatomic proofs of quantum mechanics do not reconcile with observations on the familiar "macroscopic" level of the human scale of reality, in which the bulk (quite literally) of our activity is perceived to take place. Conversely, classical physics, like Einstein's Theory of Relativity, describes the behavior of matter on a macroscopic scale, such as the trajectories of crash test dummies and space probes — but it does not explain subatomic events. For decades, physicists have searched for a Unified Field Theory or a "Theory of Everything" that would resolve these two incongruent sets of physical laws.

This incompatibility between the laws governing the macroscopic and subatomic worlds has understandably caused many scientists to question whether human perception accurately represents external reality. If the most basic particles of reality follow the strange laws of quantum mechanics, of being in multiple possible places; of being "entangled" or connected over long distances and of behaving like particles and waves, then is our experience of physical reality accurate? This is the main question being asked in *What The Bleep Do We Know?!*

INFINITE POSSIBILITY

A basic feature of quantum physics that is strongly emphasized in the film can be summed up in the statement made by Amit Goswami, Ph.D. during the first few minutes: "Quantum physics, very succinctly speaking, is the physics of possibilities."[1]

What do physicists mean when they speak of infinite possibility? A primitive description is as follows. As one may recall from High School chemistry class, the hydrogen atom consists of one proton with one electron orbiting around it.[2] This electron is so small and moving so fast that its location cannot be absolutely pinned down, moreover any attempt to locate it will alter its location. Moreover, experiments show that this electron can behave like a wave as well as like a particle; it is therefore described as having a "wavefunction" which has the "probability" of being located anywhere, at any time within the orbital shell surrounding the proton and it may show up outside of this orbital shell or even outside of "this" universe, as well. So, from a philosophical standpoint, the state of this electron could be interpreted to be one of infinite possibility.

The idea of infinite possibility occurring at the most fundamental level of physical reality can be seen to be a very liberating concept. This is certainly the view of the filmmakers of **What The Bleep Do We Know?!** The upshot of the concept of infinite possibility — and arguably a subtext of the film — is the wide-open invitation to ask the question "What if…?", or as John Lennon once sang, "Imagine."

MANY WORLDS VS. WAVEFUNCTION COLLAPSE

Infinite possibility might sound nice but it can also blow the barn doors off your head. The Many Worlds Interpretation of Quantum Mechanics proposed by Hugh Everett III in 1957 posits an infinite potentiality similar to that possessed by our wayward electron but on a universal scale; the MWI proposes infinitely replicating universes, where everything is not merely possible; it is actually happening in a parallel universe. Though it sounds totally schizoid, this idea is widely accepted in contemporary theoretical physics:

...a poll of 72 leading physicists conducted by the American researcher David Raub in 1995 and published in the French periodical *Sciences et Avenir* in January 1998 recorded the following results:

Yes, I think MWI is true	**58%**
No, I don't accept MWI	**18%**
Maybe it's true but I'm not yet convinced	**13%**
I have no opinion one way or the other	**11%**

According to Raub, supporters of MWI include Stephen Hawking and Murray Gell-Mann... Among the skeptics are Roger Penrose. Richard Feynman is also said to have accepted MWI (although obviously not in this poll, since he died in 1988).[3]

The Many Worlds Interpretation of Quantum Mechanics (MWI) discards the more conventional, previously formulated interpretation of "wavefunction collapse," a concept which attempts to describe why reality tends to appear to us as one universe, instead of as an infinite fuzzball of quantum potentials. In the MWI, every possible event is actually occurring, whether in "our" universe or in some instantaneously created parallel universe but for whatever reason, our awareness only sees the one universe it happens to be "in." Physicists who do not like the wackiness of the Many Worlds Interpretation cling to the rock of "wavefunction collapse."

In traditional Quantum Theory, the "reduction" to one universe from an infinity of possible universes is a product of wavefunction collapse. Now, if they just got rid of dorky terms like wavefunction collapse (a.k.a. "collapse of the state vector"!), then we could all be armchair physicists and feel really smart! In popular expression, "wavefunction collapse" could translate into "how the ball bounces" or "how the cookie crumbles." A quantum system is said to be in a "superposition" of possible states until it is observed; the observation causes the system to reduce (or "collapse") to a specific state. Another scientist interviewed in the film, Jeffrey Satinover, M.D., described it thus:

> A particle, which we think of as a solid thing, really exists in a so-called superposition: a spread out wave of possibilities and it's all of those at once. The instant you track on it, it snaps into just one of those possible positions.[4]

Based on statements in his published works and in the film, Fred Alan Wolf, Ph.D. subscribes to a version of the MWI. However, another scientist interviewed in **What The Bleep Do We Know?!**, Stuart Hameroff, M.D., does not agree with either the Many Worlds Interpretation or the traditional theory of universal "reduction" described above.

In the early 1990s, Hameroff teamed up with Oxford emeritus professor, Sir Roger Penrose, who is a living deity of modern physics on par with Stephen Hawking, to develop a theory of consciousness called Orchestrated Objective Reduction, in a bold attempt to unify quantum mechanics with classical physics — *and* neuroscience! Known as "OR," the theory proposes that consciousness and its associated quantum gravity *is* the wavefunction collapse between the quantum world of infinite probability and the classical world of "solidity" and it describes how "multiple universes" are thus prevented from forming. This process occurs around 40 times per second. (Their theory, which is not widely accepted in the physics community, will be discussed in more detail in a separate chapter):

> Dr. David Albert maintains that superposition is even stranger than all of the above postulations can even hint at; that all these theories are coming from our current mind-set in an attempt to make sense out of something that cannot be made sensible. "It's rather that the particle is in situation in which questions about it's position can't even be raised," says Albert, "in which questions about it's position don't even make sense, in which asking about the particle's position has the same logical status as asking about the political affiliations of a tuna sandwich like I said, or the marital status of the number five."[5]

There are many scientists interviewed in the film, with as many differing views. As Fred Alan Wolf says on his website:

> So far there are many, perhaps four main, interpretations of quantum physics currently in use. They are the Bohr collapse postulate, the Cramer transactional postulate, the Everett parallel worlds postulate, and the Bohm hidden variable postulate. They all differ in what they say the world is made of, but they all are based on the quantum physics mathematical laws describing a quantum wavefunction.[6]

Competing quantum theories currently being developed are the source of raging debate in the academic community. Because theories are not facts, these debates can quickly degenerate into a battle of belief systems and ideological predispositions. Too often, scientific debates are about what is "accepted" rather than being about science. If more people subscribe to Theory A than Theory B, then Theory A is "accepted."

CONTROVERSY AND CRITICISM: MATERIALISM VS. IDEALISM

Most scientists today are materialists, a legacy of the role of science in beating back Medieval superstitions and ignorance. Materialism is the "accepted" ideology in the world of science. However, there is a growing rift between orthodox materialists, who cozy up to this mechanistic worldview, where life is a function of the DNA molecule and where consciousness is the product of brain chemicals, and alternative thinkers, who are unsatisfied by such explanations and look towards an understanding of spirituality through modern science. *What The Bleep Do We Know?!* is about this alternative movement and most of the scientists interviewed in the film fall into the alternative category.

However, most scientists in the materialist camp HATE *What The Bleep Do We Know?!* Richard Dawkins, British author of *The Selfish Gene* and perhaps the world's most famous exponent of fundamentalist materialism, had this to say about the film a few days before the film was released in the UK:

> This film is even more pretentious than it is boring. And it is stupefyingly boring — unless, of course, you are fooled by its New Age fakery, in which case it might indeed be — as many innocent dupes have stated — "life-changing"...
> What drives me to despair is not the dishonesty of the charlatans who peddle such tosh, but the

dopey gullibility of the thousands of nice, well meaning people who flock to the cinema and believe it.[7]

Many British reviews are so scathing, they're quite funny:

Verdict: A ridiculous blend of science (fiction) and spiritualism, this facile attempt to explain the meaning of life proves to be little more than an advert for a bunch of New Age mystics. Dire.[8]

And:

Overall, if you manage to stay awake, you'll be exposed to such ludicrous extrapolations from microphysics that you may emerge expecting electrons to have vaginas.[9]

At a preview of the film at Imperial College in London, Fred Alan Wolf noted:

What's interesting…is how vehement people who respond in that way seem to be. I don't think I've had a book published without being attacked with axes…These guys are almost religious in scientific dogma. But the real big brains like Stephen Hawking and Sir Roger Penrose. They don't have any problem with this kind of thing, so why should pipsqueaks?[10]

The filmmakers' aim was to inspire the audience with a presentation of the ideas about infinite possibility and the interrelationship between consciousness and matter. Both concepts are staples of old school quantum theory and are hardly off the map. Personally, I found myself uplifted by such thoughts; that things do not have to be the way they are; that we can choose to live and to see things differently. Given the success of the film, I am apparently not alone. However, this is what a US bastion of materialism, *Popular Science* had to say about it:

> Beware: A ridiculous new science movie is coming to a theater near you. *What the #$*! Do We Know?*...If the movie even has a central message, it could best be summarized as, "We don't know #$*!"...the real shame with this film is that it plays on people's fascination with science while distorting and misrepresenting that science...Instead of stoking the curiosity of those moviegoers, *What the #$*!* numbed them with mindless quantum drivel.[11]

Fundamentalist materialists seem uniformly to have hair-trigger tempers and to take extreme delight in ridicule. What is this guy so angry about and where is his outrage every time the Discovery Channel broadcasts "Walking With Dinosaurs"? Piped into people's homes every week — into the young minds of children — this digitally animated television series of fanciful depictions based on speculations of what dinosaur life was like bears the imprimatur of science, without having to constantly fall over backwards to explain to the audience that it is entirely hypothetical.

The information in **What The Bleep Do We Know?!** could hardly be said to be destructive or mind numbing; quite arguably the opposite. Plus, none of the theoretical physics statements made by the scientists were beyond the bounds of legitimate, contemporary discussion.

What is offensive to the minds of materialists is an unflinching subscription by some of the interviewees shown in the film to a worldview that takes quantum physics to an ultimate conclusion, where objective reality does not exist, as is reflected in the statements of Jeffrey Satinover, M.D.:

> There's a physical reality that's absolutely rock solid and yet…it only comes into existence when it bumps up against some other piece of physical reality. That other piece may be us and of course we're partial to those moments but it doesn't have to be, either…it can be some incidental rock comes flying along and interacts with this fuzzy mass of stuff and sure enough, it provokes it into a particular state of existence.[12]

Perhaps the most radical physicist interviewed is Amit Goswami, Ph.D. when he says:

> Instead of thinking of things as things — we all have the habit of thinking that everything around us is already a thing, existing without my input, without my choice. You have to banish that kind of thinking. Instead, you really have to recognize that even the material world around us; the chairs the tables, the carpet — camera included — all of these are nothing but possible movements of consciousness. And I am choosing, moment-to-moment, out of those movements, to bring my actual experience into manifestation. This is the only radical thinking you need to do. But it is so radical; it is so difficult because our tendency is that the world is already out there, independent of my experience. It is not. Quantum physics

has been so clear about it. Heisenberg [1901-1976], himself, core discoverer of quantum physics, said atoms are not things, they're only tendencies, so instead of things, you have to think of possibilities. They're all possibilities of consciousness.[13]

To which *Scientific American*'s Michael Shermer says, "Okay, Amit, I challenge you to leap out of a 20-story building and consciously choose the experience of passing safely through the ground's tendencies."[14] To which Stuart Hameroff, M.D. replies, "*What The Bleep* is entertainment. Lighten up!" while at the same time skillfully defending, point-by-point, Shermer's attempts to debunk Hameroff's own Objective Reduction theory, which he formulated with Roger Penrose. Hameroff concludes, "Skeptics like Shermer should apply their craft to conventional dogma as well as to upstart hypotheses."[15]

Actually, Goswami's quote above appears to be one of several instances where the unscripted scientist interviews in **What The Bleep Do We Know?!** were edited such that the fullness of their views were not reflected, whether for reasons of timing or to fit the context of what the filmmakers were expressing at any given moment. This was partially an outgrowth of the free form, documentary style in which the scientist interviews were shot. The off-the-cuff interviews with the scientists created a dynamic climate quite different from what would have been produced in a controlled, scripted environment.

PHYSICS AND CONSCIOUSNESS

Is Amit Goswami some kind of snake oil salesman of junk science, as suggested by *Scientific American*'s

Michael Shermer? Hardly. Goswami received a Ph.D. in Physics over 40 years ago and taught physics at the University of Oregon for almost as long. Now retired from teaching, he is a Senior Scholar in Residence at the Institute of Noetic Sciences and is the author of several books. In the Foreword to Goswami's book, *The Self-Aware Universe: How Consciousness Creates the Material World*, Fred Alan Wolf writes:

> There is too much quantum weirdness around, too many experiments showing that the objective world...is an illusion of our thinking...[Amit Goswami] posits a hypothesis that is so strange to our Western minds as to be automatically dismissed as the ravings of an Eastern mystic. It says that all of the above paradoxes are explainable, are understandable if we are to give up that precious assumption that there is an objective reality "out there" independent of consciousness.

In *The Self-Aware Universe*, Goswami compares the prevailing materialistic worldview of science versus his own opposing view, where consciousness is the "ground of all being." However, this opposing view does "not deny that matter has causal potency."[16] In other words, Goswami does not deny that there would have to be some heavy-duty negotiation of some sort, between himself and the sidewalk, in order for him to emerge unscathed from a 20-story fall.

Goswami is a proponent of what he calls "monistic idealism," where mind and matter are integrally part of one reality — a reality that is not based on matter: "instead of positing that everything (including consciousness) is made of matter, this philosophy posits that everything (including matter) exists in and is manipulated from consciousness."[17]

> The philosophy that has dominated science for centuries (physical, or material, realism) assumes that only matter — consisting of atoms and elementary particles is real; all else are secondary phenomena of matter, just a dance of constituent atoms. This worldview is called realism because objects are assumed to be real and independent of subjects, us, or of how we observe them.
>
> The notion, however, that all things are made of atoms is an unproven assumption; it is not based on any direct evidence for all things. When the new physics confronts us with a situation that seems paradoxical from the perspective of material realism, we do tend to overlook the possibility that the paradoxes may be arising because of the falsity of our unproven assumption...
>
> This book shows that the philosophy of monistic idealism provides a paradox-free interpretation of quantum physics that is logical, coherent, and satisfying. Moreover, mental phenomena — such as self-consciousness, free will, creativity, even extrasensory perception — find simple, satisfying explanations when the mind-body problem is reformulated in an overall context of monistic idealism and quantum theory. This reformulated picture of the brain-mind enables us to understand our whole self entirely in

harmony with what the great spiritual traditions have maintained for millennia. [18]

In the following chapters, we will take a deeper look at the work of the physicists interviewed in **What The Bleep Do We Know?!**

CHAPTER 3
DAVID ALBERT & HOW REALITY DOES *NOT* WORK

"...the strict, soulless, external, mechanical laws of quantum theory...left us not one whit freer, not one whit more spontaneous, and not one whit more in charge of our destinies than the deterministic mechanics of Newton did."

David Albert, Ph.D.
Professor and Director of Philosophical Foundations
of Physics, Columbia University
Author of *Time and Chance and Quantum
Mechanics and Experience*

FROM DESPERATE HOUSEWIVES TO DISGRUNTLED PHYSICISTS...

The participation of David Albert, Ph.D. in **What The Bleep Do We Know!?** is most noteworthy for his very public regret over having participated in the film, at all.

Imagine if one were a respectable professor at an Ivy League university, who had been interviewed by a crew of bright-eyed, indie filmmakers — and to have afterwards seen oneself spliced together with Ramtha...one might well have hit the ceiling! My guess is that Albert's reaction to the film was due to his being one of the only interviewees who wasn't already down with "the Ram."[1]

Prior to their involvement with **What The Bleep Do We Know!?**, Fred Alan Wolf, Candace Pert, John Hagelin, Joe Dispenza and Miceal Ledwith had all spoken and sold books at the Ramtha School of Enlightenment in Yelm, Washington (the latter two appear to be RSE employees). After a flurry of negative reviews came out, claiming that *What The Bleep* was a recruitment film for Ramtha, Marlee Matlin issued a statement that she did not know who Ramtha was prior to making the film but that she did not believe the film unduly promoted RSE. The other scientists probably thought it best to keep mum about the whole thing and to let the film's popularity and its attendant controversy work for them.

But Albert was hopping mad that his views contradicting the filmmakers' belief in the New Age credo, "You Create Your Own Reality" were cut from his interview, complaining that he was "…unwittingly made to sound as if (maybe) I endorse [the film's] thesis."[2]

He went on a media blitz, stoking the polemic in *Willamette Week*:

> Philosopher David Albert, who runs the Philosophical Foundations of Physics program at Columbia University, says the filmmakers totally misrepresented him. "They must have filmed me for four hours," he told *WW*. "It became clear to me they believe that…by positive thinking we can alter the structure of the world around us. I spent a long time explaining why that isn't true, going into great detail. But in the movie, my views are turned around 180 degrees."[3]

…and setting the record straight in *Popular Science*:

> David Albert, a philosopher of physics at Columbia University, is outraged at the final product. He

says that he spent four hours patiently explaining to the filmmakers why quantum mechanics has nothing to do with consciousness or spirituality, **only to see his statements edited and cut to the point where it appears as though he and the spirit warrior [Ramtha] are speaking with one voice**. "I was taken," Albert admits. "I was really gullible, but I learned my lesson."[4]

Albert's statements in *Salon.com* reveal perhaps the key reason for his distress:

...I was edited in such a way as to completely suppress my actual views about the matters the movie discusses. I am, indeed, profoundly unsympathetic to attempts at linking quantum mechanics with consciousness. Moreover, I explained all that, at great length, on camera, to the producers of the film... Had I known that I would have been so radically misrepresented in the movie, I would certainly not have agreed to be filmed. **I certainly do not subscribe to the 'Ramtha School of Enlightenment,' whatever that is!**[5]

"180 DEGREES..."

My hunch is that Albert was at least as upset about the Ramtha association as he was about any misrepresentation of his views, especially since he wrote a book in 1992, *Quantum Mechanics and Experience*,[6] in which he speculated about the role of consciousness in the production of "reality," or as it is known in quantum physics jargon, "wavefunction collapse":

...perhaps the collapse occurs precisely at the

> last possible moment; perhaps it always occurs precisely at the level of consciousness, and perhaps, moreover, consciousness is always the agent that brings it about.

And:

> The brain of a sentient being may enter a state wherein states connected with various different conscious experiences are superposed; and at such moments the mind connected with that brain opens it's inner eye and gazes on the brain, and that causes the entire system (brain, measuring instrument, measured system, everything) to collapse...

It appears that Albert's views might have turned around 180 degrees in the years since he published those statements and it is a testament to the filmmakers' integrity that they invited Albert to speak at the *What the Bleep* conference in Santa Monica, California in February 2005, where he was encouraged to air his disagreement with the film's premise and to let everyone know what he thinks is true *now*:

> Thank you very much. It's a privilege to be with you all today. I think that what we're involved in is important, here. I think that the film we're here to talk about raises large and urgent and fundamental questions about science and about truth and about what it is to be human and about where the culture is headed...

> I am very grateful to have been invited to tell you what it is that bothers me and that saddens me about all that...

As for the speculations about the role of consciousness, the speculations which are at the very center of *What The Bleep*, they disappeared from the serious scientific and philosophical literature a good thirty years ago [i.e., fifteen years BEFORE he wrote *Quantum Mechanics and Experience*]. Insofar as physics and philosophy are concerned, they belong to fairly ancient history. Moreover, even if those speculations had turned out to be right, the world would look nothing at all, frankly, like the picture we're presented in *What The Bleep*.

There's never been a serious suggestion in the physical literature...that quantum mechanics [means] somehow that, "I create my own reality," that, "I choose what I experience," that there's room in the world for the quote intangible phenomenon of "freedom," as somebody says in the film. **Insofar as anybody has ever entertained the possibility that consciousness counted as an active agent in the quantum mechanical world, it was understood that every last detail of the operations of that agency would need to be governed by the *strict, soulless, external, mechanical laws of quantum theory...those laws left us not one whit freer, not one whit more spontaneous, and not one whit more in charge of our destinies than the deterministic mechanics of Newton did.***

It seems to me that what's at issue...between serious investigators of the foundations of quantum mechanics and the producers of *What The Bleep* is very much of a piece of what was at issue between Galileo and the Vatican and very much of a piece of what was at issue between Darwin and the Victorians: **there's a deep and perennial and profoundly human impulse to approach the world with a demand...with a condition that what has got to lie at the center of the universe...at the foundation of all being, as somebody puts it in the film, is some powerful and reassuring and accessible image of ourselves.**

That's the impulse that *What The Bleep*, it seems to me, seems to flatter and to endorse — *and perhaps even to exploit*. And *that*, more than any of its particular factual inaccuracies, *is what bothers me about it*. The business of resisting that demand, the business of approaching the world with open and authentic wonder and with a *sharp, cold eye* — and singularly intent on the truth — is called science. (Huge applause).[7]

I wish I could convey the spectacular lack of affect in Albert's delivery of these words, as he compared the film's producers to the Vatican, of all things. In print, his words appear quite fiery and passionate, compared to how he spoke them. Albert's truth is very much the "sharp, cold eye" he describes. He insists on the fundamental mechanicality of the universe and on the idea that we are organic automatons, with no ability to choose our destinies. What he now says about consciousness is that it: "is an enormous and profound, unexaggeratably important puzzle about the world."[8]

THE KNIGHT OF TP

Albert is the opposite of another disgruntled physicist,

the illustrious (and hotheaded) Sir Roger Penrose, in an unrelated matter. When the Knight saw his proprietary five-fold symmetric tiling pattern, which had taken him years to solve by hand because they belonged to an arcane set of "non-computable" problems that could not be calculated by computer — *embossed on rolls of toilet paper*, he filed a lawsuit against the manufacturer, Kimberly-Clark Corporation. He also demanded that all existing stock of the plagiarized TP be confiscated and destroyed and that an inquiry be made into Kimberly-Clark's profits so that the damages could be properly assessed:

> ...Widely known in the geometry field as "Penrose tilings," this particular pattern is notable for using only two polygons to cover a surface. A thin diamond and a thick one form an endlessly interlocking field of five-pointed stars and decagons...Backing Penrose in his lawsuit is Pentaplex Ltd., a company that licenses Penrose tilings and other of Sir Roger's creations for use in puzzles and games.

> "So often we read of very large companies riding rough-shod over small businesses or individuals," said David Bradley, director of Pentaplex. **"But when it comes to the population of Great Britain being invited by a multi-national to wipe their bottoms on what appears to be the work of a Knight of the Realm without his permission, then a last stand must be made."**[9]

It is hard to say who is wackier — Sir Roger or Ramtha? Alas, Penrose's case didn't have a leg to stand on because his pattern is most significant for never repeating itself. The mass-produced toilet paper design most certainly did repeat itself (though Kimberley Clark was kind enough to discontinue the batch).

THE QUANTUM AUTOMATON

It's a pity, too that it ended up this way for Dr. Albert. He could have played nice with the *What The Bleep* crowd and peddled his version of reality and been on his way to becoming a quantum physics pop star, like Fred Alan Wolf. But Albert is a rigorously precise academic, his ivory tower sensibility utterly violated by the New Age showbiz flair of some of his colleagues — and quite possibly, by the very concept of sales, itself. Albert will not likely be caught dead on a Quantum Cruise.

Here is some more vintage Albert, in a seminal 4-page paper that he wrote, "On Quantum-Mechanical Automata," which influenced the work of Fred Alan Wolf and was cited by many others. In it, he appears to be suggesting that human awareness might be a scaled-up version of the mechanical behavior of a *quantum automaton*. An automaton is the heart of a "sequential machine" (the method established by John Von Neumann in the 1940s to conceive single units of computations), which deals only with inputs and states:

> If a quantum-mechanical automaton were (in a particular way) to look at itself and measure itself and produce a description of itself, that description would be different, not just in content but in *nature*, from any description it might produce of an external object; and such a state of affairs as that has no precedent and no analogue among classical automata.

> One cannot think of such things without

thinking of the many-worlds interpretation of quantum mechanics (to put it another way: one cannot ask such questions without, in the back of one's mind, asking a more difficult one; **whether such an automaton might be a model of our own empirical experience**). [10]

Fred Alan Wolf based his model of self-reflective quantum physical neural states in part on Albert's theoretical work, in his paper, "On The Quantum Mechanics Of Dreams And The Emergence Of Self-Awareness"[11] which was edited by another scientist familiar to us, Stuart Hameroff, M.D. However, unlike the filmmakers of *What The Bleep Do We Know!?*, Wolf was careful to point out that his interpretation of Albert's theory would not necessarily be agreeable to him…

CHAPTER 4
JEFFREY SATINOVER, M.D. &
THE QUANTUM BRAIN

"...the stuff of life is a 'machine' only in the way that quantum mechanics is 'mechanical' — shot throughout with uncountable numbers of uncaused events, possibly taking place in a nearly infinite number of cross-talking parallel universes..."

Jeffrey Satinover, M.D. (Psychiatry), M.S. (Physics)
Past President of the C.G. Jung Foundation of New York
William James Lecturer in the Psychology of Religion,
Harvard University
Author of several books, including *The Quantum Brain*
and *Cracking the Bible Code*

LABELS

Critics of **What The Bleep Do We Know!?** disapprove of the vocational fence-jumping of the interviewees, implying that if you are not paid to be a quantum mechanic, then you should not be discussing the subject on camera.

However, most car mechanics make better money than quantum mechanics, so people with these skills often do something else to make a living. In Stuart Hameroff, we have a practicing anesthesiologist who formulated a Unified Field Theory with Oxford University Emeritus Professor, Sir Roger Penrose and in Jeffrey Satinover, M.D., we have a psychiatrist who gives some of the most easy-to-understand mini-lectures about quantum physics in the film.

Satinover is good at this because he has been teaching introductory physics at Yale, where he received a master's degree in physics as a member of the Theoretical Condensed Matter Physics group. He is working toward his Ph.D. at the Laboratoire de Physique de la Matière Condensée at the University of Nice, Sophia Antipolis, studying the prediction of chaotic time series, with applications to biological systems, climate change and markets.

Is Satinover "less than" as a scientist, as some critics would seem to suggest? Let's see. A look at his bio says he's been a psychoanalyst since 1976 and received his medical degree to begin practicing psychiatry in 1986. His books have been published in nine languages. He engineers computer programs that produce statistical, neural-network and genetic-algorithm investment models, which he does as a partner at a hedge fund in Westport, Connecticut.

The guy is Mr. Achievement, not to mention an intellectual omnivore: He teaches Constitutional Law as a Visiting Lecturer at Princeton; he is a director of The Durckheim-Gladstone International Center for Quantitative Analysis in Washington, D.C.; he holds degrees from MIT (S.B.), Harvard (Ed.M.), the University of Texas (M.D.) and Yale (M.S.); he completed psychoanalytic training at the C.G. Jung Institute of Zürich; he is a former fellow (resident) in psychiatry and child psychiatry at Yale, where he was twice awarded the department of psychiatry's Seymour Lustman Residency Research Prize (2nd place); he was the 1975 William James Lecturer at Harvard...

This is not even the tip of the iceberg of what Satinover has accomplished and continues to do,[1] yet he had the integrity and humility to say during the final credit roll of the film:

> I should make it clear that I am a graduate student in physics and not a full-fledged theoretical physicist yet but that if fortune smiles on me and if I continue to work like a dog on my problem sets and exams and whatnot, eventually what I hope to do with this is to apply fundamental quantum theory to quantum information processing.

This comment was an opening for critics to assail the panel of scientists interviewed in *What The Bleep Do We Know!?* as "so-called experts." If critics had done their homework, they might have considered that Satinover may be better qualified to discuss any number of scientific topics than ten movie critics put together.

In Boulder in April 2005, Satinover started off his talk at the *What The Bleep* conference with a joke that he was currently in a race against Alzheimer's to get his Ph.D. in condensed state matter physics. He explained that although he had been a practicing psychiatrist most of his career, he had a lifelong interest in physics and that he had not appreciated the opportunity with which he had been presented at age 13, when Richard Feynman was his mentor.

Satinover went on to recount how, during the Santa Monica conference in February 2005, he had gotten to play "good cop" because David Albert was there and had been given free reign to voice his dissent over the interpretation of quantum physics that had been emphasized in *What The Bleep Do We Know!?*. Satinover said that Albert's untoward rant had allowed him to play nice in Santa Monica but because Albert would not be appearing at the Boulder event, he would be forced to play the "bad cop" and would have to express his disagreements over the film's presentation of quantum physics. Satinover said he had discussed his disagreements with Producer-Director Will Arntz, who had shown himself to be non-dogmatic and willing to correct himself and said that he considered Arntz to be "an intelligent and good guy." The audience burst into applause.

He then asked the audience how many of them understood the basics of quantum physics (this was after two straight days of quantum physics lectures). Out of an audience of 500, approximately five people raised their hands. He then asked how many of these understood these principles before the conference and the same five people kept their hands up. From what seemed to be a genuine sense of wanting to provide the audience with what they needed, he proceeded to break it down for the audience.

What I saw was a man who radiated integrity, humility, kindness and thoughtfulness. However, this view was seriously shaken by what I later discovered to be another one of his big achievements: Satinover has succeeded in becoming the bane of Gay Rights activists worldwide!

EX-GAY MOVEMENT ADVISOR AND ANTI-PORN EXPERT WITNESS?

What?! Among the many other things that this busy man does, Satinover is an advisor to the National Association for Research and Therapy of Homosexuality and he is apparently on the payroll of conservative mega-think tank, The Heritage Foundation for the creation of a:

...fully cross-linked international database of medical, social science and legal citations with associated metanalyses and aggegrated data tables. The purpose of the database is to assist concerned scholars, attorneys, social scientists, policy analysts and citizens worldwide in addressing the nearly-universal problem of the embedding in legal documents of gross distortions (or even wholesale inventions) of social science conclusions to make ideologically-driven alterations in public policy appear rationally based.[2]

Presumably, the purpose is to undermine attempts by Gay Rights groups to push legislation based on purportedly bogus scientific studies. His book, *Homosexuality and the Politics of Truth*, equates homosexuality with addiction; as a destructive behavior, which he believes can be treated and "cured."

This is a whole can of worms that is off the subject of Satinover's work in **What The Bleep Do We Know!?**, in quantum physics and perhaps beyond the purview of this book, but it would be remiss for it to go unmentioned. With his 20 years of clinical practice and evidence that he is a highly intelligent, deeply thoughtful and well-intentioned person, my guess is that he really believes this stuff and is not merely on the take for conservative payola. It seems fair enough that if there are people suffering out there, who want help with their "unwanted same-sex attractions," then they should be able to get it and their rights should be protected. However, it is important to note that:

"Ex-gay" programs have been denounced by

every respected medical and mental health care organization and child welfare agency in America, including the:

American Psychiatric Association, American Psychological Association, American Medical Association, American Academy of Pediatrics, American Association of School Administrators, American Federation of Teachers, The Interfaith Alliance Foundation, National Academy of Social Workers, National Education Association, American Counseling Association, World Health Organization, Council on Child and Adolescent Health.[3]

It appears that the filmmakers were quite intent on generating controversy over their choice of interviewees — and Ramtha wasn't enough! Speaking of whom, since nearly all the scientists interviewed in the film appear to be part of the RSE curriculum, I cannot help but wonder whether Satinover got on the filmmakers' radar because of JZ Knight's and/or Ramtha's views on homosexuality. JZ's late ex-husband, Jeffrey, struggled with his own homosexuality and sadly succumbed to AIDS after their divorce:

...papers from Knight's 1992 divorce case with Jeffrey Knight hint that Ramtha is an ancient homophobe, who allegedly declared that AIDS was Mother Nature's way of "getting rid of" homosexuality...[4]

The weirdness doesn't stop here. On November 18, 2004, Satinover appeared as an expert witness on the dangers of Internet pornography before the Senate Commerce

Committee's *Science, Technology and Space Subcommittee* (love the venue!), saying:

> Pornography really does, unlike other addictions, biologically cause direct release of the most perfect addictive substance. That is, it causes masturbation, which causes release of the naturally occurring opioids. It does what heroin can't do, in effect.
>
> The Internet is dangerous because it removes the inefficiency in the delivery of pornography, making porn much more ubiquitous than in the days when guys in trench coats would sell nudie postcards.[5]

…your tax dollars at work, folks…

MAN IS A MACHINE

OK, that was fun. Let's talk about Satinover's *The Quantum Brain: The Search For Freedom and the Next Generation of Man.* This book is not an easy read but it does have lots of remarkable accounts from the history of mathematics and computers. He gets into the future of computers, which is incredibly interesting but I will limit my discussion to the important points he makes about how quantum physics occurs in life processes and how he thinks this tends to disprove the mechanistic view of reality and everything in it, including the human race.

Satinover talks about John Von Neumann's view that physical reality and all the phenomena of life, from embryo development to the formation of neural networks in brain architecture, are just different kinds of cellular automata, i.e., the fundamental building blocks of digital processing, "...computation ('processing') is something that nature (life especially) performs just by doing what it does..."[6]

> From a computation perspective, physical reality is inherently like a cellular automaton, and thus facilitates computation and self-organization at all scales...From a mathematical point of view, neural networks and cellular automata are almost identical — only the physical basis and appearance are different: Self-organization at one scale yields the capacity for self-organization at the next.[7]

Satinover says that the scientific evidence that man is machine is overwhelming:

> To explain what we are and what we can do requires no appeal to anything beyond the natural potentials of dumb matter acting locally...Everything that constitutes us and our existence is simply what mechanically had to be. There were no choice points in the processes that produced us; there are no options in the actions we take: The road not taken is nothing but a road impossible to take. There is nothing preventing us from generating — from forcing the evolution of alternate forms of "us," because there is nothing about us that sets us apart from mere mechanicality.[8]

As unappealing — or liberating — depending on your taste, as this may seem, the above is essentially the worldview of most scientists, David Albert being a good example.

However, puppy dog-hearted Satinover says that there may be a way out of this classical materialist point of view, a view which is perfectly — even gleefully — summed up in a statement made by Richard Dawkins: "The universe we observe has precisely the properties we should expect if there is, at bottom, no design, no purpose, no evil and no good, nothing but blind, pitiless indifference."[9]

QUANTUM PHYSICS TO THE RESCUE!

> There exist structures in the human brain that appear perfectly designed to capture quantum effect and amplify them via chaos...If so, the actions generated by the brain, and of human society as a whole, would share at least some of the absolute freedom, mysteriousness, and nonmechanicality of the quantum world.[10]

You can see here, that where Albert views quantum laws as mechanistic, Satinover (among others) feels quite the opposite. Satinover tells how the idea of life being a quantum phenomenon grew out of similarities observed between the behavior of quantum particles and the behavior of living entities — especially of humans. He notes that Poincaré, Heisenberg, Pauli, among others have remarked on how the "decision" of quantum particles to show up "wherever they wanted" seemed so much like "free will." If the behavior of quantum particles was truly caused by nothing, while living systems (such as humans) were supposedly machines, then couldn't it be argued that atomic particles have free will and humans do not?

> Ever since quantum mechanics was first appealed to (by its inventors) as having some mysterious connection to life in general and

to human freedom in particular, skeptics have derided such claims, as we've seen. Quantum events have nothing whatsoever to do with biology at even a microscopic scale, they argue, let alone with actions on the human scale...a 100 percent mechanical system cannot under any circumstances generate an indeterminate outcome...**should human beings be shown to have any capacity whatsoever to act other than in accord with rigid, mechanical determination, that capacity would therefore either have to derive from the quantum nature of matter, amplified, or arise from some other, utterly mysterious source.**[11]

Satinover asserts that human beings, especially their nervous systems and brains, function as *quantum amplifiers*, "amplifying internal quantum events upward." The brain's self-organizing, parallel processing iterative structure is that of an automaton, where the final outcomes of each scale constitute the initial states of the next scale. He says that the brain could hardly have been better designed to be a quantum amplifier, though he warns that, "this amplification...does not allow one to witness large-scale aggregates of living matter obeying quantum rules, as pop quantum mysticisms propose,"[12] (his own footnote for this statement cites books by Fritjof Capra, Fred Alan Wolf and Danah Zohar).

Satinover explains how incredibly complex protein molecules are formed by living bodies, folding into various *conformational states* at breakneck speeds, with almost no waste of energy. The way they are able to do this is by taking advantage of *quantum tunneling*. The definition of quantum tunneling is when a particle travels faster than the speed of light through a barrier (i.e. another particle), even when it does not have the energy required to do so (per classical physics). Citing the work of Stuchebrukhov,[13] he says that certain protein structures called "bridges" enhance electron tunneling along multiple, widely separated, superposed paths.

> In other words, for a time a portion of the protein is in a superposed state that involves substantial distances. Furthermore, superposed quantum paths can interfere. This is utterly impossible for point-like electrons transferring along some kind of fixed "highway" and leads to effects not present in any classically mechanistic view of biological processes — including unexpectedly long-distance quantum tunneling.[14]

Not just electrons, but entire hydrogen atoms have been found to tunnel through very large, lattice-shaped protein molecules, especially in certain enzyme actions. Quantum tunneling effects are observed in water and DNA molecules, as well. He posits that all of this is mounting evidence that the concept of man as machine is rather dubious. "...the stuff of life is a 'machine' only in the way that quantum mechanics is 'mechanical' — shot throughout with uncountable numbers of uncaused events, possibly taking place in a nearly infinite number of cross-talking parallel universes..."[15] He states furthermore of proteins, "...the quantum properties are intrinsic, classically impossible and almost certainly necessary for life to be possible at all."[16]

GOD

In the last chapter of his book, entitled "God," Satinover talks about a sea change now occurring in the world of science, as a result of quantum mechanics. Where it has previously been taboo for scientists to even mention God, let alone profess faith in such a thing, that attitude is beginning to change.

In the view of Satinover and others (though certainly not of Albert and the majority of scientists), the relentless experimental confirmation of quantum mechanical theory has dealt death blows to the mechanistic, deterministic worldview. Quantum teleportation, quantum computation and quantum cryptography are not only being taken seriously, corporations are throwing big bucks into their research and development:

> It is a world in which one can comfortably argue the dynamics of interference among multiple universes both forward and backward in time; can ask seriously, as did Feynman and Wheeler, whether every electron in the universe is the same one, just reappearing through multiple loops in time and be doubted but not derided…Well, in that kind of world, it is in some ways less of a stretch to speak of God.[17]

Satinover, who practices Orthodox Judaism, says it is a matter of preference how one explains the quantum foundational basis of the universe: "Either it is absolute chance or absolute will. Opposite as they sound at first, between the two science can point to no distinction and the universe, it seems, will offer no evidence."[18]

He says that the only camp deserving of fierce opposition is the one that allows for itself no serious possibility that it might be wrong, which he says includes as many materialists as religious fundamentalists. He also expresses his opinion that if we do not root ourselves in the wisdom that gave birth to our culture, we will destroy ourselves.

Although I might not agree with all of his politics, I cannot help but come away with a lot respect for Satinover's active mind and vast interdisciplinary learning.

CHAPTER 5
STUART HAMEROFF, M.D. &
ORCHESTRATED OBJECTIVE REDUCTION

*"I make my living as an anesthesiologist and every day,
as I put my patients to sleep, I kind of wonder where
they go..."*

Stuart Hameroff, M.D.
Professor of Anesthesiology & Psychology
Associate Director of the Center for Consciousness Studies,
University of Arizona
Author of several books, including *Toward a New Science
of Consciousness I & II*

ANESTHESIOLOGIST/PHYSICIST?

Some viewers of **What The Bleep Do We Know!?** may
be wondering why an anesthesiologist was up there
talking about quantum physics. This is because Stuart
Hameroff, M.D. is not your average anesthesiologist. He
is an anesthesiologist who has devised a Unified Field
Theory — in conjunction with a theory of consciousness
— together with Oxford University Emeritus Professor of
Physics, Sir Roger Penrose.

In person, Hameroff comes off the smartest man on the
planet; the most articulate and the swiftest debater — and
he has a great sense of humor, too. He gets so little screen
time that one does not get any sense of this in the film.
Based on what I have seen of Hameroff's written work and
his talk at the *What The Bleep* conference in Boulder, I wouldn't
be surprised if everything else he said on camera was so
heady that it was deemed unusable by the filmmakers.

After studying chemistry, physics and mathematics as an undergraduate, Hameroff went to medical school, where the mechanical, yet seemingly intelligent movements of cell structures during cell division fascinated him. The structures that interested him the most were the cylindrical protein assemblies called microtubules, whose crystal lattice array reminded him of a computer switching circuit. He began asking himself during the early 1970s if these microtubules could possibly be processing information the way computers do?

Advances in electron microscope technology allowed Hameroff to see that brain cells were particularly rich in these microtubules. This supported his hunch that these microscopic structures might be related to the "problem" of consciousness, as this mystery is called by science.

Though his interests lay chiefly in neurology and psychiatry, Hameroff was convinced by Professor Burnell Brown to join the faculty of the Department of Anesthesiology at the University of Arizona, where he had just completed his medical internship. Citing a paper showing that anesthetics caused microtubules to disassemble, Brown suggested that knowledge of the complex chemical reactions involved with general anesthesia was the most direct route to solving the riddle of consciousness. Hameroff began his practice as an anesthesiologist, while continuing his investigations into microtubules, publishing several papers and a book in 1987, *Ultimate Computing: Biomolecular Consciousness and Nanotechnology*. He also co-founded The Center for Consciousness Studies at The University of Arizona in the early 1990s.

After reading *The Emperor's New Mind*, Hameroff contacted its author, renowned Oxford University physics professor emeritus, Roger Penrose to discuss his ideas with him:

> Roger had turned to the problem of consciousness and concluded the mind was more than complex computation. Something else was necessary, and that something, he suggested, was a particular type of quantum computation he was proposing ("objective reduction" — a self-collapse of the quantum wave function due to quantum gravity). He was linking consciousness to a basic process in underlying space-time geometry — reality itself!... Roger didn't have a good candidate biological site for his proposed process...I wrote to him, and we soon met in his office in Oxford in September 1992. Roger was struck by the mathematical symmetry and beauty of the microtubule lattice and thought it might indeed be the optimal candidate for his proposed mechanism. Over the next few years...we began to develop a model for consciousness involving Roger's objective reduction occurring in microtubules within the brain's neurons. Because the proposed microtubule quantum states were "tuned" or "orchestrated" by linking proteins, we called the process "orchestrated objective reduction" — 'Orch OR' which has engendered a lot of interest and severe criticism.[1]

This chapter will attempt to explain Objective Reduction in the simplest terms and the implications of this theory, which Hameroff and Penrose concocted together.

ORCHESTRATED OBJECTIVE REDUCTION

Dissatisfied with the prevailing scientific view of consciousness as no more than a biological form of computation, Penrose argued that nerve cells are too big to be the source of consciousness; that consciousness must be a subatomic phenomenon. The premise of the "Orch OR" model is that consciousness may be explicable with the application of quantum theory:

> ...a physical "theory of everything" should at least contain the seeds of an explanation of the phenomenon of consciousness. It seems to me that this phenomenon is such a fundamental one that it cannot be simply an accidental concomitant of the complexity of brain action...[2]

As discussed previously, the traditional view of how quantum wavefunctions "collapse" or "reduce" into the classical state of seemingly solid, "linear" phenomena is called *subjective reduction*. In this model, collapse can occur either by conscious observation, measurement or environmental "entanglement," resulting in a statistical projection of the given particle's location.

Not liking this fuzzy outcome one bit, Penrose proposed that a new physical ingredient was needed: Objective Reduction, in which coherent quantum systems can "self-collapse" upon reaching a critical mass/time/energy threshold related to *quantum gravity* (see definition in following paragraph). In this scheme, the results of collapse do not have to be random, but can reflect a quantum computation (a superposition of information bits which interrelate by non-local entanglement), occurring in a state of quantum coherence (a state of balance when two or more particles' individual frequencies are in constructive interaction, i.e. are "in sync"):

> ...in the Penrose-Hameroff model, consciousness does not *cause* collapse of the quantum wave function (*à la* Copenhagen). Rather, consciousness *is* collapse. More precisely, consciousness is a particular type of self-collapse proposed by Penrose involving quantum gravity (currently being tested). Pre-conscious (unconscious/subconscious) information exists as quantum superpositions — multiple coexisting possible actions or experiences — which, upon reaching a specified threshold at the moment of consciousness/self-collapse, choose a particular action or experience. Such conscious moments are calculated to occur roughly 40 times per second.[3]

Quantum gravity describes the interaction of gravity with the three other fundamental forces of *electromagnetism*, the *strong nuclear force* and the *weak nuclear force*. Gravitation is the tendency of masses to be attracted to each other. Electromagnetism is the physics of the electromagnetic field. Both the strong and the weak nuclear forces are short-range forces, limited to distances shorter than the nucleus of an atom. The residual effects of the strong nuclear force bind neutrons and protons together in the nucleus of an atom. The weak nuclear force has a field strength that is 109 times weaker than the strong nuclear force and is present in radioactive decay.

> But what is consciousness? According to the principles of OR (Penrose, 1994), superpositioned states each have their own space-time geometries. When the degree of coherent

mass-energy difference leads to sufficient separation of space-time geometry, the system must choose and decay (reduce, collapse) to a single universe state, thus preventing "multiple universes" (e.g. Wheeler, 1957). In this way, a transient superposition of slightly differing space-time geometries persists until an abrupt quantum classical reduction occurs and one or the other is chosen. Thus consciousness may involve self-perturbations of space-time geometry.[4]

SUBJECTIVE REDUCTION VS. OBJECTIVE REDUCTION

In the traditional quantum theory of subjective reduction, a system is in a superposition of possible states until observed, causing it to collapse; in objective reduction, the superpositioned states each have their own bubble-like space-time geometries, which are unstable and will self-collapse into one particular curvature/separation when the warping of these space-times reaches an objective quantum gravity threshold. The larger the bubble-like separation/superposition, the faster it will self-collapse — and the more intense the conscious experience, because in the objective reduction model, consciousness is seen to be an aspect of wavefunction self-collapse, via quantum gravity.

Microtubules are made up of tubulin molecules. The Penrose-Hameroff model proposes that internal quantum events occurring within tubulins, in cooperative interaction with each other, are the bridge between subatomic quantum events and molecular, "classical" reality. Each self-collapse corresponds with a distinct conscious event, which occur on average 40 times per second:

...microtubule subunits (tubulins) are coupled to internal quantum events, and cooperatively interact (compute) with other tubulins. We further assume that macroscopic coherent superposition of quantum-coupled tubulin conformational states occurs throughout significant brain volumes and provides the global binding essential to consciousness. We equate the emergence of the microtubule quantum coherence with pre-conscious processing which grows (for up to 500 milliseconds) until the mass-energy difference among the separated states of tubulins reaches a threshold related to quantum gravity.

Sequences of such events create a stream of consciousness. The objective reduction is "tuned" by the cell's microtubules and is thus self-organized, or "orchestrated":

Possibilities and probabilities for post-reduction tubulin states are influenced by factors including attachments of microtubule-associated proteins (MAPs) acting as "nodes" which tune and "orchestrate" the quantum oscillations.[5]

In addition, "pre-conscious" information is seen to be encoded in space-time geometry at the fundamental Planck scale. Different kinds of conscious experiences correspond to various configurations of quantum spin geometry. Consciousness, as we know it occurs when a self-organizing process (the objective reduction) accesses these pre-conscious states.

Fellow *Bleep* interviewee, Jeffrey Satinover criticizes the Penrose-Hameroff model as improbable because it requires that 20,000 neurons at a time exist in a single *coherent* quantum superposition for one fortieth of a second, which is an enormous amount of time at the quantum level. He says: "...in spite of Penrose's genuinely stellar reputation and contributions to physics and mathematics (only Einstein himself has contributed more to the Theory of General Relativity) — *Shadows of the Mind*[6] was quickly assigned to the growing heap of pop physics and consciousness books that few scientists take seriously."

A WORD FROM THE ÜBER-SKEPTIC

Michael Shermer, founding publisher of *Skeptic Magazine* wrote a flaming review of *What The Bleep Do We Know!?* for *Scientific American* magazine, in an article entitled "Quantum Quackery." Although Shermer calls the Penrose-Hameroff model the "best candidate" to "link the weirdness of the quantum world to mysteries of the macro world (such as consciousness)":

> In reality, the gap between subatomic quantum effects and large-scale macro systems is too large to bridge. In his book *The Unconscious Quantum* (Prometheus Books, 1995), University of Colorado physicist Victor Stenger demonstrates that for a system to be described quantum-mechanically, its typical mass (m), speed (v) and distance (d) must be on the order of Planck's constant (h). "If mvd is much greater than h, then the system probably can be treated classically." Stenger computes that the mass of neural transmitter molecules and their speed across the distance of the synapse are about two orders of magnitude too large for quantum effects to be influential. There is no micro-macro connection.

Then what the #$*! is going on here? [7]

Which seemed like a reasonable enough claim. However, Hameroff responded:

> To debunk our theory Shermer cites an assertion in a book by Victor Stenger that the product of mass, velocity and distance of a quantum system cannot exceed Planck's constant. I've not seen this proposal in a peer reviewed journal, nor listed anywhere as a serious interpretation of quantum mechanics. But in any case Stenger's assertion is disproven by Anton Zeilinger's experimental demonstration of quantum wave behavior in fullerenes and biological porphyrin proteins. (Skepticism should cut both ways, Mr. Shermer.) Nonetheless I agree with Stenger that synaptic chemical transmission between neurons is completely classical. **The quantum computations we propose are isolated in microtubules within neurons.** Classical neurotransmission provides inputs to, and outputs from, microtubule quantum computations mediating consciousness in neuronal dendrites. [8]

Shermer and Jeffrey Satinover both quibble about biological temperatures being too high for quantum states, the latter saying, "the 'randomizing' effects of heat (thermal agitation of the tubulins) was not taken into account, as if they were operating at absolute zero, which is biologically unrealistic." [9] But Hameroff has a comeback for these concerns, as well:

> But the brain seems far too warm for significant

quantum states, apparently running into the problem of decoherence. **(Shermer conflates the strong Copenhagen interpretation of the measurement problem — that conscious observation causes wave function collapse, with decoherence — in which any exchange of energy or information with the environment erodes a quantum system.)** But recent evidence shows that quantum processes in biological molecules are actually enhanced at higher temperatures. Moreover biological mechanisms within neurons (actin gelation, laser-like metabolic pumping, plasma layer shielding and topological quantum error correction in/around microtubules) may preserve quantum states in microtubules for hundreds of milliseconds or longer at brain temperature.

...and here, Hameroff shows how his expertise in anesthesiology has given him a unique insight into the chemical and subatomic interactions involved in human consciousness:

Is there any evidence for the relevance of quantum states/processes to consciousness? Well, general anesthetic gases selectively erase consciousness while nonconscious brain activities continue (e.g. evoked potentials, control of autonomic function, EEG). **The anesthetic gases act in the same intra-protein non-polar pockets in which quantum London forces control protein conformation. This occurs in a class of receptors, channels and other brain proteins including cytoskeletal structures. And the anesthetics** do so by forming only quantum mechanical interactions, presumably interfering only with physiological quantum effects. It is logical to conclude that consciousness occurs in quantum pockets within proteins throughout the brain.

Shermer also conflates the Copenhagen interpretation with the dualist quantum mind proposal of Sir John Eccles...

Shermer closes by advising researchers to look for emergence of consciousness at the neural level and higher. This has been precisely the tack taken by armies of scientists and philosophers for decades, and the result is nil. Consciousness is ever more elusive. The prevalent paradigm — that axonal action potentials and chemical synaptic transmissions are fundamental units of computation from which consciousness emerges at a higher-order network level — force-fits consciousness into an illusory, out-of-the-loop epiphenomenon. While this might be true, the prevalent paradigm is also incompatible with the best electrophysiological correlate of consciousness — synchronized gamma EEG ("coherent 40 Hz" oscillations). The latter, it turns out, is mediated by coherent activities of neuronal dendrites linked by electrotonic gap junctions, windows which link adjacent neurons (and glia) into large-scale syncytia, or "hyper-neurons."[10]

I didn't completely understand the last sentence — and I hope the reader didn't throw the book at the wall just now! All know is that Hameroff is smarter and scrappier than most.

Satinover cites the paper by Stuchebrukhov, where quantum tunneling effects were observed by entire hydrogen atoms traveling through huge protein molecules and where entire portions of protein molecules exist in a quantum, superposed state. It therefore does not seem like a ridiculous stretch to me that, "consciousness occurs in quantum pockets within [tubulin] proteins throughout the brain," as Hameroff asserts. The Penrose-Hameroff model certainly seems more plausible than the cloddish idea that consciousness is a "product" of chemical reactions in the brain…

CRANKS AND PRANKSTERS

In short, the Penrose-Hameroff model is an interesting, if unusual marriage between an absolutely mechanistic vision of consciousness with a dash of Platonic idealism:

> I'm not an idealist, like Bishop Berkeley or Hindu approaches, in which consciousness is all there is. Nor am I a Copenhagenist in which consciousness causes collapse (and chooses reality from a number of possibilities). But somewhere in between. Consciousness exists on the edge between the quantum and classical worlds. I think more like a quantum Buddhist, in that there is a universal proto-conscious mind which we access, and can influence us. But it actually exists at the fundamental level of the universe, at the Planck scale.[11]

According to the online encyclopedia Wikipedia, the Penrose-Hameroff model "…is widely considered a crank view…" Hameroff affirms that they have been continuously attacked ever since they published their model in 1994/5:

> …but [we] are still kicking, generating testable predictions which thus far have held true…the conventional wisdom proponents are more interested in protecting their turf than honestly considering alternatives. But it's much better to be criticized than ignored. On the other hand skepticism is good (there are a lot of whacky ideas floating around — I just think ours is not one of them). But the skeptics should be as skeptical of the conventional dogma, which is extremely weak. The title of Roger's book *The Emperor's New Mind*, aimed at artificial intelligence (or maybe specifically at Marvin Minsky), was the perfect example. Roger called their bluff. AI is naked, haughty and pretentious when it comes to the question of consciousness.[12]

I completely agree with Hameroff's statements about the scientific orthodoxy, however I must admit that, in the course of my attempts to translate the cryptic jargon of the "Orch OR" model into English for this chapter, I could not help but be reminded of the Bogdanoff Affair of 2002, where it was rumored that twin brothers, Igor and Grichka, had succeeded in publishing at least five papers of pure gobbledygook in physics journals as a hoax (though the twins continue to deny this) — and had actually received Ph.D. degrees in physics on the basis of this bogus work! There was lots of hand wringing in the physics community and the media had a field day, joking that theoretical physics was so divorced from reality that not even the experts could recognize the difference between real work and a hoax:

> Until then, few physicists had noticed the
> brothers' theses or their journal articles,
> which purport to exploit something called the
> Kubo-Schwinger-Martin condition. It implies
> a mathematical connection between infinite
> temperature and imaginary time (don't ask)
> to probe the state of the universe at its very
> beginning. Suddenly physicists were trying to
> figure out what sentences like this meant, if
> anything: "Then we suggest that the (pre) space-
> time is in thermodynamic equilibrium at the
> Planck-scale and is therefore subject to the KMS
> condition."[13]

This is in no way to disparage the work of Hameroff and
Penrose, which I consider to be a valiant effort to unify
classical and quantum physics and a plausible model of
consciousness. I only bring up the Bogdanoff saga in
the spirit of fun, since my own experience of reading
Hameroff's paper was a grueling rendezvous with my
own ignorance!

I am no physicist, while Sir Roger Penrose most certainly
is, not to mention one of the most respected on earth.
What he has to say speaks volumes about what the bleep
we do NOT know:

> ...there is at least one glaring omission in present
> physical theory. This is how small-scale quantum
> processes can add up, for large and complicated
> systems, to the almost classical behaviour of
> macroscopic bodies. Indeed, it is not just an
> omission but an actual fundamental inconsistency,

sometimes referred to as the measurement paradox (or Schrödinger's cat). In my view, until this paradox is resolved we must necessarily remain very far from a physical theory of everything — whether or not such a theory exists.[14]

Beyond the Bleep

CHAPTER 6
FRED ALAN WOLF, PH.D. & *THE YOGA OF TIME TRAVEL*

*"The real trick to life is not to be in the know —
be in the mystery."*

Fred Alan Wolf, Ph.D.
Physicist, lecturer and writer
Author of several books, including *The Yoga
of Time Travel* and *Taking the Quantum Leap.*

WALKING HIS TALK

In reading through Wolf's peer-reviewed scientific papers and the popular physics books he writes for an avid lay readership, one cannot help but come away with admiration for this affable ambassador of quantum physics. When the film opened in the UK in May 2005, Wolf fielded the crusty orthodoxy with aplomb:

> You have to hand it to the distributors; it was brave putting on a preview the other night at Imperial College in London, a temple of straight, white-coated science…The college cinema was full, with about a 70/30 split between students and staff and New Age fans. **It was received with a mix of open-mouthed horror and ecstatic approbation**, the approbation winning out, but coming mostly from what seemed to be committed fans. There were mumbles of "bullshit" from one or two clumps of students…

The highlight was a question-and-answer session with Dr. Fred Alan Wolf, one of the film's stars, owner of a splendid array of Einstein hair and a CV (including being professor of physics at San Diego State University for 12 years) that should be enough to silence sceptics, but wasn't...

Dr. Wolf got a bit testy when a scientist said, "I find the science very disturbing, full of half-truths and misrepresentations. And I suspect the majority of working physicists will find the film offensive." **Seeming to believe Dr. Wolf was an actor, the voice went on to bet him £10,000 that no scientist would back *What The Bleep*. Dr. Wolf countered by explaining as modestly as possible that he has written 11 books on quantum [physics] and counter-bet that 10 years from now, his interlocutor will believe things he currently regards as preposterous...**[1]

With all the nasty swipes made by science writers regarding *What The Bleep Do We Know!?*, we have not seen any published attacks directed against Wolf and there are no rabid Ph.D.s on Internet message boards trashing him, either — probably because he is such a nice guy! He is the Teflon physicist, who for over twenty years has managed to purvey his blend of quantum physics, anthropology and spiritualism without stirring up the bile of the orthodoxy. Wolf may be the real star, if not the major inspiration for this film, but "Rumors that Burger King will have a Fred Alan Wolf doll are not true,"[2] jokes William Arntz, the film's Co-Director and Producer.

With a knack for making the most abstract hypotheses accessible to the amateur, Wolf sells the reader on the unity between two trendy themes in today's pop culture: yoga and time travel. What he ends up delivering is a crash course in the transpersonal teachings of Eastern mysticism and his take on cutting edge theories of quantum physics.

He begins his latest book, *The Yoga of Time Travel: How the Mind Can Defeat Time* by showing that many concepts found in ancient and Eastern spiritual traditions are compatible with contemporary physical theory, pointing to the old legends which say that time is the progenitor of the cosmos and that time itself is the child of consciousness.

> Digging deeper into the ancient texts, we find that they say time and space are products of the mind and do not exist independent of it. The principles of quantum physics, remarkably, tell us the same thing. This is an extraordinary key. The trick to going outside the confines of space and time is to reach beyond their source — the mind itself. Paradoxically, we need a theoretical picture created by the mind to understand what it means to reach beyond the mind...

> In the early part of the first millennium BCE, Indian philosophers found evidence for the beginnings of what we today call the perennial philosophy. It can be stated in three sentences:

> 1. An infinite, unchanging reality exists hidden behind the illusion of ceaseless change.

> 2. This infinite, unchanging reality lies at the core of every being and is the substratum of the personality.
>
> 3. Life has one main purpose: to experience this one reality — to discover God while living on earth.[3]

Hinduism's *Bhagavad Gita* is said to teach a way to understand what is *real*. Its fundamental lesson is that detachment is the way to enlightenment. Wolf's own interpretation of quantum physics shows that the processes of attachment and detachment are deeply related to the way time works through the mind, speculating that *time and consciousness are two different names for the singular process by which we become attached to material existence*. He suggests that once we recognize what causes our attachment to the everyday world of matter and causality, we can detach ourselves from its confines — and thereby defeat time.

Yoga is the Hindu school of philosophy where the ultimate aim of the practitioner is to merge consciousness with the *one common soul*, a.k.a. "God," through a rigorous practice of meditation, metaphysics and devotion. The way to achieve this is by the dissolution of the ego, as laid out by the *Yoga Sutras* of Patanjali, written around 2500 years ago. The fully realized yogi who is able to attain this state of awareness will purportedly display evidence of "superhuman" abilities:

> knowledge of past and future, including past and future lives; the ability to "read" other people's minds — even precise details of thought; full awareness of the ways consciousness works; the ability to become invisible; and even the ability to levitate.[4]

Coming back to the theme of time travel, Wolf suggests that the key to unlocking one's ability to do it is to be willing to "leave some luggage behind" — namely, one's ego. He suggests this can eventually be accomplished by meditating on the idea that you are not your body, as well as by perfecting the yogic postures known as the *asanas,* which are used to bring the mind to concentration and absorption: "...By becoming fully conscious of the body, the practitioner realizes that he or she is *other than the body* and merges with the soul."[5]

SPONTANEOUS TIME TRAVEL

Losing the ego to escape the temporal realm sounds like a lot of work but there is scientific evidence that the human brain accesses the quantum field on a routine basis. An experiment conducted in 1976 by Kolers and Grünau[6] indicated that people's awareness, quite literally went back in time. When a red dot was projected onto a wall and then and a split second later, a green light projected slightly to the right of it, the persistence of vision caused test subjects to see a light moving as a line across the wall, switching in color from red to green halfway across its trajectory. Not only was the linear movement of the light from left to right an illusion, the subjects all reported that the light switched from red to green *before* the green spot ever appeared on the wall!

> Does the brain act like a time machine, projecting the experiences back in time?...Clearly, the illusion of the switch of color at the illusory midpoint cannot occur until *after* the second spot registers in some way in the brain. So the mind must look forward in time, see the green color, and then back up in time to make the switch...It turns out that the forward motion of time is an illusion rooted

> deeply in the Western psyche, founded on one
> single concept — that time is linear.[7]

Citing the work of physicist John G. Cramer,[8] Wolf says that the laws of physics do not forbid time travel but may actually require it. Moreover, according to the laws of the *time reversal invariant*, even old school classical physics has no problem with events appearing in reversed time order.

POSSIBILITY WAVES

Wolf describes how "*possibility*-waves" provide a connection between sub-reality to reality by means of the simple mathematical operation called *squaring*, which changes these subreality waves into reality probability curves, which form the very basis of the cause-and-effect world that appears to us as "reality."

Infinite possibilities overlapping are called a *superposition* in quantum physics jargon. Wolf has coined the term "*possibility*-wave," which would be a sub-unit of a superposition of possibilities. (He says he italicizes the word "*possibility*" to underscore its mysteriousness). The conventional view, put forth by Niels Bohr (1885-1962) is that the "*possibility*-wave" squares itself, producing a probability curve when an observation occurs — but as yet, no one has fully explained how this happens. To answer this question, physicist John G. Cramer proposed that to calculate the probability of an event, the *possibility*-wave must be multiplied by a time-reversed mirror image of the original wave, known as the "complex conjugate."

> Thus the conjugate *possibility*-wave travels in
> the opposite spatial direction as it goes back
> through time, eventually reaching the original
> *possibility*-wave's origin…at every point along its

way, it meets up with the original wave coming forward in time. The two then combine in space...the conjugate wave is said to "modulate" the original wave [similar to the way TV signals modulate or piggyback on the carrier frequency in TV transmissions]...

[Frequency modulation] is nothing more than the product of two waves multiplied together. Since the waves are almost identical in form, this multiplication is, in effect, squaring. In order for any event to occur, both quantum waves must be simultaneously present, one modulating the other. As Cramer explains it, when the future-generated conjugate propagates back through time to [meet] the origin of the quantum wave itself...the two waves multiply [in space and time] and the result is the creation of the probability-curve for the event occurring in space and time.

Cramer calls the original wave an "offer" wave, the conjugate wave an "echo" wave, and the multiplication of the two a "transaction"...an offer wave is sent to a receiver. The receiver accepts the offer and sends confirmation back along the same line...

Every observation is both the start of a wave propagating toward the future in search of a receiver-event and itself the receiver of a wave that propagated towards it from some past event...every observation — every act of conscious awareness — sends out both a wave toward the future and a wave toward the past...

> Which future event sends back the echo wave?
> Cramer believes that only one future does this
> — the one producing the echo that happens
> to have the best chance of forming a successful
> transaction with the present. [9]

Wolf's elaboration of Cramer's theory is to say that the
function of the mind is one of *converting possibility*-waves
into probability-curves by performing this squaring
operation, thus producing probabilistic outcomes in the
real world. Whereas, Cramer believes that the only future
that sends back the echo wave is the one that has the
best chance of connecting with the present, Wolf's view
is in line with the Many Worlds hypothesis, in which it
is not just the best-chance future but rather an infinity
of futures (a.k.a. parallel worlds) which each contain a
single future event that connect with the present event
through the modulation effect. Once the modulation
takes place, the parallel worlds split off and no longer
interfere with each other.

> [If this theory is real,] time must not be like a
> one-way river after all. Events that have passed
> must still be around. Events that will be must
> exist…and if both the future and the past exist,
> then, quantum physics implies, devices must be
> feasible that can enable us to tune into the future
> and resonate with the past. These devices seem
> to be our own brains, with our minds [as] the
> controlling factors… [10]

A REALITY CHECK FROM MY SECRET
QUANTUM PHYSICIST ADVISOR…

…and just when quantum physics was starting to get
really fun, my anonymous physicist advisor tells me

that Cramer's theory is *not real*...

> Wolf is accepting what Cramer is saying without any attempt of analyzing whether it makes sense or not. A detailed analysis of Cramer's idea is available on my other blog: Open System for Geniuses.[11] Cramer is making an elementary error of assuming that quantum mechanics is about waves travelling in a physical space, rather than about "state vectors" and "density matrices" in a Hilbert space — see for instance, "Density State" in Wikipedia...
>
> There is no "complex conjugation" operation in a Hilbert space — contrary to what Cramer suggests. Unitary time reversal operation may exist — but has nothing to do whatsoever with the scalar product that is being used for calculating "probabilities" (except that it is "anti-unitary," like many other operators). But physics professors do not like to criticise other physics professors. Why? Because these other professors could reciprocate, and who is without any sin?[12]

Although Wolf maintains that: "In [Cramer's] transactional interpretation, the wave is real; it exists in real space and time; before and after the collapse,"[13] in a personal email to me, my advisor counters:

> That sentence shows lack of elementary understanding of quantum mechanics. In quantum mechanics, the wave function is not in real space and time but in the "configuration space" that is $3N$ dimensional, where N is the

number of particles. So, for 10 particles the wave function is in 30-dimensional space. See e.g. [this paper][14] where another interpretation of the quantum theory is discussed that Wolf does not know about, but which is quite popular: GRW spontaneous localization. In September 2005 there will be a conference on this subject (that is "quantum jumps") in Trieste[15]

I am planning to go there, so I will probably meet David Albert who will speak there about philosophical problems of quantum mechanics.

It would be very interesting to know Wolf's response to these assertions, since he surely has more than an "elementary understanding of quantum mechanics." Interested readers are encouraged to visit my physicist advisor's two blogs[16] and to trudge through the theoretical physics papers and websites he cites in order to better understand why my secret advisor thinks the Wolf-Cramer model as well as other claims by some physicists in *What The Bleep Do We Know!?* are rather pie-in-the-sky…

MIND YOGA, TIME TRAVEL, PARALLEL UNIVERSE "THERAPY" AND MAGICK

Despite these withering criticisms from my physicist friend, we will continue our synopsis of Wolf's thoroughly engaging book: Quantum physics points to something preceding space, time and matter. Wolf calls it sub-spacetime; others have called it the imaginal realm; Goswami calls it a transcendent, nonmaterial, archetypal domain of *potentia*; Hameroff calls it a "universal proto-conscious mind which we access, and can influence us…[it] exists at the fundamental level of the universe, at the Planck scale"; and Roger Penrose has described it as an "idealistic" reality, akin to Plato's world of ideas. In present-day quantum theory it is conceived as "infinitely dimensional space."

Wolf tells of an old physics homily that says, "whatever is not forbidden becomes compulsory" and how in the past decade, there has been a big shift in the scientific attitude toward time travel. Where the burden had previously been on physicists to prove that time travel was possible, now the burden has become to prove there is a law forbidding it!

Wolf believes that consciousness plays a role on the most fundamental level of matter and that yoga and meditation can help people develop their ability to focus and unfocus — and thus affect the squaring and unsquaring of *possibility*-waves, opening the door to new possibilities in the world of manifestation. As an exercise to heal one's past, one could train one's awareness on a focal point where *possibility*-waves from the past meet and merge with *possibility*-waves from the present moment, thus squaring and producing a new probability-curve; this could be a kind of parallel universe "therapy." Likewise, awareness could be trained on a focal point where *possibility*-waves from the future meet and merge with *possibility*-waves from the present, magnetizing an event to one's present, as a kind of parallel universe magick:

> I know it is nearly unthinkable, and perhaps seems even ridiculous to entertain such notions but the past is not fixed in spite of our present memories. Each time a switch takes place reconnecting to a new past parallel universe with the present universe, history changes as we remember it, and we emerge in the new parallel universe with memories now consistent with it.

However, for big changes to be made in the past involving parallel universes, my research suggests that many people would be needed. It works like a hologram: the more area of the hologram being illumined, the stronger the "signal" and the greater and more real becomes the image. Smaller changes — individual changes — can be accomplished individually or in a small group.[17]

Wolf describes human consciousness as sequences of triplets: defocusing, focusing and defocusing, which is why perception of reality tends to blur and spread out after a focused moment. Through focusing and defocusing, time is created, making time travel intrinsic to the way that mind functions and the way time works. In Wolf's view, time and mind can have the same meaning:

...the importance of consciousness as an element in physics is becoming apparent, and the link between time and consciousness has been forged. The seat of consciousness — the soul or essential self —now appears to be directly involved with time, possibly with its very emergence as something we think we can objectify... Consciousness acts or has an effect on physical matter by making choices that then become manifest. It now appears that such an action cannot simply take place mechanically. Implied now is a "chooser," or subject who affects the brain and nervous system. Some physicists, such as [Henry] Stapp, believe that this chooser arises in the brain through past conditioning. [Roger] Penrose believes the action of choosing takes place nonalgorithmically — that is, not through the action of any mathematical formula or any computer-like process. I suggest that this chooser/observer does not exist in spacetime and is not material, which suggests that it is a spiritual essence or being residing outside of spacetime.[18]

If you were worried that Wolf's book was getting a little too spiritual for the nuts 'n' bolts, classical physics-type guys, he trots out some quantum computers and a HUGE piece of time travel hardware.

Columbia University's David Deutsch pioneered the theory of quantum computers in the 1980s and 1990s and they are now being researched in several laboratories around the world, although Wolf predicts that they will not be a reality in the average home for another ten years. The microchip technology of today's computers follows quantum laws but users of the foreseen quantum computers will also have the ability to tap into the bizarre quantum world. "Just what this will mean...remains to be seen. Whatever it means, the world will be stranger indeed, and device-assisted time travel may indeed become a reality."[19]

> The remarkable thing about quantum computers is that they operate in parallel universes! Thus a quantum computer and its clones, each in its separate world, carry out parallel calculations... You not only get to use the results of one computer's work, you get the results from an infinite number of them. To get our time machine working, we need to get the parallel-universes quantum computers working in harmony with each other, so that their outputs produce a special superposition of number possibilities. Let me call this special superposition "state-S."[20]

AHARONOV'S TIME TRAVEL SPHERE

The time travel device envisioned by Israeli physicists Yakir Aharonov and Lev Vaidman is one in which the traveler would move either backward or forward in time while the rest of the universe remained the same. The subject would be placed inside of a massive spherical shell, which in order for the laws of classical general relativistic time dilation to occur, would have to be at least the size of a small planet or large satellite, because it would need to possess enough gravity in order for time to slow down around it.

To amplify the effect of the sphere's mass and radius, a quantum computer would be connected to the sphere, set to the special parallel universes superposition "state-S," causing the sphere to split and enter each parallel world that the quantum computer would be in, with a slightly different radius. In principle, a time shift as large as desired could be produced. When the time traveler exited the device, he would experience reality in his new state. Apparently, even without the quantum computer attachment, a small amount of shift could occur from gravity alone, depending on the size of the shell, "the smaller the radius and the greater the mass, the greater the shift...[I]ncrease the radius or decrease the mass, and the time shift decreases."[21]

Aharanov and Vaidman had found a way to get the universes to coalesce into a single universe by making the quantum computer enter a new state, which Wolf calls "state-T," which like state-S, would be a special superposition of number possibilities different from state-S. All of the possible time shifts would be superposed together, yielding one major time shift; the time traveler would move significantly forward or backward in time, in accordance with the programmed state-S. The success of this experiment would depend on how often one could make a quantum computer change from state-S into the special overlap state-T, in which these small time shifts could add together to produce a giant time shift.

Aharanov and Vaidman admitted, however that its probability would be so rare that it would hardly ever happen...!

Wolf explains that this hypothetical time shift would relate to shifting the time traveler's *possibility*-wave. Being inside the large sphere, the time traveler's *possibility*-wave could be severely distorted by a large enough time shift. For travel to the past, the machine would actually shift the *possibility*-wave of the time traveler to a possible past of his, in which he had been isolated from the world-at-large. In other words, it would be an alternate or *counterfactual* past of his. It is speculated that such a device could one day be used to wipe out bad memories and to cure illnesses, by taking to the subject back to a point in time prior to the negative events occurring...

CHAPTER 7
AMIT GOSWAMI, PH.D. & MONISTIC IDEALISM

*"...We are at the center of the universe
because we are its meaning."*

Amit Goswami, Ph.D.
Professor Emeritus of Physics, University of Oregon
Senior Scholar in Residence, Institute of Noetic Sciences
Author of several books, including *Self-Aware Universe*
and *Physics of the Soul*

QUANTUM PHYSICS AND METAPHYSICS

One physicist interviewed in *What The Bleep Do We Know!?*
expresses views which are so antithetical to what is
accepted by both Western science and commonsense that
his statements have become a lightning rod for the film.
Amit Goswami has been slapped around in the press like
some kind of low rent huckster of airy-fairy junk science,
not as the emeritus professor of physics with over three
decades of university tenure that he is in actuality:

> The film's avatars are New Age scientists whose
> jargonladen sound bites amount to little more
> than what California Institute of Technology
> physicist and Nobel laureate Murray Gell-
> Mann once described as "quantum flapdoodle."
> University of Oregon quantum physicist
> Amit Goswami, for example, says in the film:
> "The material world around us is nothing but
> possible movements of consciousness. I am
> choosing moment by moment my experience.

> Heisenberg said atoms are not things, only tendencies." Okay, Amit, I challenge you to leap out of a 20-story building and consciously choose the experience of passing safely through the ground's tendencies.[1]

Perhaps some of the abuse he incurred may have been avoided, had he been permitted to expand on his ideas some more. If one reads Goswami's book, *The Self-Aware Universe: How Consciousness Creates the Material World* it becomes clear that his fascinating hypotheses were not fully explained in the film, which is understandable, since they are quite complex, deserving a documentary all their own. In this chapter, we will take a look at the revolutionary ideas put forward in his book and how these views were distorted in the film, if inadvertently.

In the following provocative quote from his interview in the film, Goswami appears to be toeing the classic, 1980s-style New Age party line about how "You Create Your Own Reality":

> In the old thinking, I can't change anything because I don't have any role in reality — reality is already there, it's material objects moving in their own ways…and mathematics determines what they will do in a given situation…I, the experiencer have no role, at all. In the new view, yes mathematics can give us something; it gives us the possibilities that all these movements can assume…but it cannot give us actual experience that I'll be having in my consciousness. I choose that experience — and therefore, literally I create my own reality. It may sound like a tremendous, bombastic claim by some New Ager without any

understanding of physics whatsoever but really, quantum physics is telling us that.[2]

Whether his statements in the interview were cut out of context or not, Goswami's use of the terms "I" and "consciousness" in conjunction with his hypotheses are very different from their everyday use, which would certainly be the meanings inferred by the unwitting viewer. To understand what Goswami really means in the above statement, one must either read his works or the digest of *The Self-Aware Universe* in the following pages.

QUANTUM PHYSICS AND THE DEMISE OF MATERIAL REALISM

In his book, *The Self-Aware Universe: How Consciousness Creates the Material World*, Amit Goswami begins by establishing the basic assumptions of the present-day Western scientific worldview, which he describes as rooted in the philosophy of material realism. This view "assumes that only matter...is real; all else are secondary phenomena of matter, just a dance of the constituent atoms. This worldview is called realism because objects are assumed to be real and independent of subjects, us, or of how we observe them."[3]

Goswami explains how modern materialism grew out of the division between mind and matter proposed by 17th Century French philosopher, René Descartes. He suggests that this division was a tacit political arrangement; Descartes would avoid attacking religion, which would henceforth be allowed to "reign supreme in matters of the mind, in exchange for science's supremacy over matter."[4] However, because science became so successful at predicting and controlling the environment, this Cartesian dualism was eventually ousted by the current "materialist monism" now ruling science, which holds that all things in the world, including mind and consciousness are made of matter. Goswami cheekily points out, however that:

> **the principles of material realism are metaphysical postulates. They are assumptions about the nature of being, not conclusions arrived at by experiment.** If experimental data are discovered that contradict any of the postulates, then that postulate must be sacrificed.[5]

Indeed, the findings of quantum mechanics have seriously destabilized the main tenets of materialism: 1) The sacrosanct ideal of *objectivity* has been shown to be inextricably bound up with subjectivity, such as when observation causes subatomic wave packets to "collapse" into localized particles; 2) the concept of *causal determinism* is destabilized by the uncertain, probabilistic behavior of particles; 3) *locality* and the idea that objects exist independently of one another is disproved by phenomena such as *quantum entanglement*, whereby particles which are spatially separated by vast distances faithfully mirror each other's behavior; 4) the materialist belief in the *epiphenomenalism* of mind, i.e. that mind is nothing but a product of chemical reactions is untenable if it is agreed that observation/measurement is what collapses a spread-out wave of a quantum object into a localized particle — or as Goswami says, **"it seems impossible that an epiphenomenon of matter could act on the very fabric of which it is built — in effect, causing itself."**[6] He finishes his discussion of the "old view" thus:

> ...The axioms of material realism...served us well in the past when our knowledge was

more limited than it is today, but now they have become our trap. We may have to let go of... certainty in order to embrace the freedom that lies outside the material arena.[7]

THE PHILOSOPHY OF MONISTIC IDEALISM

The monistic idealism that Goswami supports is not new, though his particular interpretation of quantum physics by means of monistic idealism is. He points out that that the most influential proponent of this philosophy in Western culture was ancient Greek philosopher, Plato (427-347 BCE). The stream of monistic idealism can be seen in virtually all esoteric traditions, as well as in the exoteric traditions of Hinduism and Buddhism.

	Manifest Reality	**Transcendent Reality**
Taoism	Yin	Yang
Hinduism	Rupa	Nama
Buddhism	Nirmanakaya	Sambhogakaya
Kabbalah	Theogony	Alma-de-Peruda
Christianity	Earth	Heaven

He explains how monistic idealism is the complete antithesis of material realism because it is consciousness and not matter that is considered to be the fundamental matrix of reality, governing both the world of matter and the world of mental phenomena. "In addition to the material and mental spheres (which together form immanent reality or the world of manifestation), idealism posits a transcendent, archetypal world of ideas as the source of material and mental phenomena." He notes that the Taoist symbol of Yin and Yang may be the most well known symbolization of the complementary immanent and transcendent realms. "It is important to recognize that monistic idealism is, as its name implies, a unitary philosophy; any subdivisions, such as the immanent and the transcendent, are within consciousness. Thus consciousness is the only ultimate reality."[8]

> Just as ordinary matter consists ultimately of submicroscopic quantum objects that can be called the archetypes of matter, let us assume that the mind consists ultimately of the archetypes of mental objects (very much like what Plato called ideas). I further suggest that they are made of the same basic substance that material archetypes are made of and that they also obey quantum mechanics. Thus quantum measurement considerations apply to them as well.

> I am not alone in this speculation. [Carl] Jung intuited decades ago that psyche and matter must ultimately be made of the same stuff.[9]

Because he posits consciousness as the "ground of all being," Goswami's hypotheses are necessarily considered to be metaphysics, albeit from the point of view of a physicist. "The brain-mind is a dual quantum system/ measuring apparatus. As such it is unique: It is the place where the self-reference of the entire universe happens. *The universe is self-aware through us.* In us, the universe cuts itself in two — into subject and object."[10]

The most important distinction to understand here is the difference between consciousness and mind. In the idealist model proposed by Goswami, the human mind is the locus of the interaction of both classical and quantum systems. In monistic idealism, *consciousness* is the "ground of all being" otherwise known as God, which would correspond to the "quantum self." However, minds are things that belong to human beings and would correspond to the "classical self." In monistic idealism, material objects (such as a ball) and mental objects (such as a thought of a ball) are both objects in consciousness. The conscious experience of this consciousness within the human mind is known as the Holy Spirit in Christianity or in Quaker Christianity, as the "inner light." Hindus refer to it as the Atman. (This experience is fairly uncommon for the average Westerner).

Therefore, the "You" in the "You Create Your Own Reality" of New Age lore is not the separate "you" that you normally think of as you; this "You" would instead be your transpersonal or divine aspect. In other words, he says your ego is not and cannot be the ultimate "Creator" of your reality/universe (Goswami is in surprising agreement with materialist determinists on this particular point, saying: "...the ego's free will is a sham").

> ...our consciousness is ultimately unitive and is at the transcendent level, which we now recognize as the inviolate level. From inside physical space-time (from the point of view of the classical programs of our brain-mind), however, we become possessed by individual identity: ego...the limitedness arises from accepting the point of view of the learned programs causally acting on one another. In ignorance we identify with a limited version of the cosmic subject; we conclude, I am this body-mind.

> As the real experiencer (the nonlocal consciousness) I operate from outside the system — transcending my brain-mind — that is localized in space-time — from behind the

> veil of the tangled hierarchy of my brain-mind's systems. My separateness — my ego — only emerges as an apparent agency for the free will of this cosmic "I," obscuring the discontinuity in space-time that the collapse of the quantum brain-mind state represents.[11]

According to monistic idealism, objects are already in consciousness as primordial, transcendent, archetypal possibility forms. The collapse consists not of doing something to objects via observing but of choosing and of recognizing the result of that choice.

IDEALISM AND THE RESOLUTION OF A QUANTUM QUAGMIRE

Monistic idealism proposes an elegant resolution to the messy and wasteful implications of the Many Worlds Interpretation of Quantum Mechanics, in that it considers quantum waves or coherent superpositions to be real — but existing in a *transcendent, nonmaterial* domain, as formless archetypes of matter.

> Suppose that the parallel universes of the many-worlds theory are not material but archetypal in content. Suppose that they are universes of the mind.[12] Then, instead of saying that each observation splits off a branch of the material universe, we can say that each observation makes a causal pathway in the fabric of possibilities in the transcendent domain of reality. Once the choice is made, all except one of the pathways are excluded from the world of manifestation.

> Behold how this way of reinterpreting the many-worlds formalism gets rid of the costly

proliferation of material universes.[13]

Goswami proposes that the universe exists as formless *potentia* in myriad possible branches in the transcendent domain, becoming manifest only when observed by conscious beings. "If this sounds as if we are re-establishing an anthropocentric view of the universe then so be it. The time and context for a strong anthropic principle has come... *We are at the center of the universe because we are its meaning.*[14]

The sticky question soon becomes, "If reality consists of ideas ultimately manifested by consciousness how do we explain so much consensus?" Goswami is quick to point out that his view is not solipsistic (where the self is the only reality), explaining that the phenomenal world looks overwhelmingly objective to us for two reasons. First of all, classical bodies have huge masses, which means that their quantum waves spread rather slowly. The small spreading makes the trajectories of the center of the mass of macro objects very predictable (whenever we look, we find the moon where we expect it), thus producing an aura of continuity. He says additional continuity is imposed by our own brain-mind's perceptual apparatus.

> Perhaps the most confusing of the self experiences are those that involve choice and/ or free will... Traditionally, behaviorists and cognitivists would say that there is no choice or free will... The argument is simply that there is no causal power that can be attributed to the ego, whose behavior is completely determined by the state of its hardware and by its inputs from the environment... *Spiritual and transpersonal psychologies would agree with the behavioral assessment that the ego does*

not have free will, but they would insist that there is free will. It is free will of the atman — the consciousness that exists before any kind of reflective, individual-self experience. If the ego does not have any free will, how do we in our ego go beyond ego, which is the objective of spiritual traditions?[15]

QUANTUM SPIRITUALITY

The idealist science proposed here does not exclude either subjectivity or objectivity, either spirit or matter; it integrates the deep dichotomies of human experience. Goswami asserts that in our illusion of separation, we have missed the simple truth that all is God, which is the mystic's way of saying all is consciousness. He notes that physics explains phenomena, but consciousness is not a phenomenon; rather, all are phenomena in consciousness. "In the most celebrated of Biblical myths, Adam and Eve live an enchanted life of wholeness in the Garden of Eden. After eating the fruit of knowledge, they are expelled from that enchantment. The meaning of the myth is clear: The price of experience in the world is a loss of enchantment and wholeness."[16]

Wholeness may have been lost but it can be regained, this presumably having been achieved by the likes of Gautama Buddha and Jesus Christ, which Goswami says, is most likely what the latter was referring to when he said, "I and my father are one." Drawing on his own Hindu background, Goswami discusses that system's different levels of "enlightenment," i.e. freedom from the illusion of separation, as well as the many ways this can be pursued, especially by the practice of meditation.

The reward for moral action is indeed heaven, but not in the afterlife. Heaven is in this life;

it is not a place but an experience of living in quantum nonlocality...what is sin?...In a quantum view, the only sin is the fossilizing of the self or others in classical functioning, to block one's own or another's access to the quantum modality and the manifestation of freedom and creativity. (This is entirely consistent with the Christian idea of original sin as the separation from God.) **For condoning the stasis, we do end up in hell – the hell-on-earth of ego-bondage**...[17]

BLINDSIGHT

Not everything in Goswami's book is metaphysical. He includes data from various particle physics and biological experiments which support his ideas, such as the results of a delayed choice experiment, proposed by renowned physicist John Wheeler, in which photon particles retroactively responded to the choice of the observer.[18] He goes on to describe the work of Nick Humphrey and Lewis Weiskrantz[19] in their "blindsight" experiments where, in an unusually cruel trial, they removed the cortical areas connected with vision from two monkeys, who were able to recover their vision (it turns out that there is a secondary pathway for optical stimuli from the retina to a structure in the hindbrain called the superior colliculus). In another experiment involving a human subject with blindsight,[20] Nick Humphrey recorded instances of unconscious perception — perception without awareness of it. He also describes another experiment conducted at the University of Oregon in 1983 by a graduate student named Tony Marcel in psychologist Michael Posner's group, who reported some cognitive data on unconscious seeing: "...the data are completely in agreement with consciousness collapsing the quantum state of the brain-mind when we see consciously. *In unconscious seeing, there is no collapse*, and that really made a lot of experimental difference."[21]

> ...**experiments [proving telepathy] have been carried out in many different laboratories and positive results are claimed with both psychic and non-psychic subjects**.[22&23] Then why has telepathy not yet been recognized as a scientifically plausible discovery? One reason from the scientific point of view is that the data on extrasensory perception (ESP) are not strictly replicable — only statistically so. There is a related apprehension that if ESP were possible, we would be able to somehow to transfer meaningful messages through it, a prospect that would create havoc in the orderly world of causality. **The most important reason for the skepticism about ESP, however, may be that it does not seem to involve any local signals to our sense organs and hence is forbidden by material realism.**[24]

OLD HABITS

Old habits die hard. Although quantum mechanics has long since replaced classical physics as the fundamental theory of physics, the idealist implications of quantum mechanics are repugnant to most contemporary physicists, who remain steadfast adherents of the materialist worldview:

> They do not want the embarrassing metaphysical questions raised by quantum mechanics. They hope that if such problems are ignored, they will go away...

A strict adherence to an idealist metaphysics, one based on a transcendent, unitive consciousness collapsing the quantum wave, resolves in a nonarbitrary fashion all the paradoxes of quantum physics. We shall find it completely possible to do science within the framework of monistic idealism. The result is an idealist science that integrates spirit and matter. **The idea that consciousness collapses the quantum wave was originally proposed by John Von Neumann in the 1930s. What took us so long to take this idea seriously?**[25]

CHAPTER 8
YCYOR: DO YOU CREATE YOUR OWN REALITY?

> The most intriguing concept in *What the Bleep*
> — and in Ramtha's teachings — is the idea that
> quantum mechanics is the ultimate proof that
> the universe is a sort of metaphysical putty we
> shape with our minds.[1]

The film's pervasive "You Create Your Own Reality"
message is the self-assured rejoinder to its exasperated
title. In an interview with *Salon.com*, the film's financier and
Co-Director, William Arntz, spoke about communicating
this prototypical New Age tenet to the audience:

> **Arntz:** It's the idea that you create your own reality
> and that there is an interface between mind and
> matter, as quantum physics suggests. We don't
> quite understand it all yet, but it seems to be there.
> That sort of idea is very huge. We're getting away
> from Newton and Descartes, where the world was
> set up with a physical universe "out there" and
> our minds have no interface with it...We're saying
> exactly the opposite. We happen to the universe.
> **We create the universe; we spin it out from
> what's inside of us. And that's a completely 180-
> degree turn. It has a lot of ramifications as to
> how people live their lives and how they react
> to so-called external events.**[2]

"You Create Your Own Reality" is an idea that promises
ultimate human fulfillment and achievement by means

of absolute self-responsibility. It is an idea that seeks to break the chains of self-limitation imposed from both without and within. Even if YCYOR is not entirely true, it can be a refreshing outlook...

The cognitive psychology component of YCYOR is certainly true enough: one's beliefs will help determine one's choices and will inform one's experiences; changing one's beliefs can radically change one's life. Yet, one cannot help but think the statement to be a bit simplistic, especially when "substantiated" by quantum mechanics. Indeed, some people find this catch phrase to be downright objectionable — though true believers of YCYOR will say that such negativists are defending their own "victim consciousness." What YCYOR fundamentalists will rarely discuss is that Jesus Christ, Mahatma Gandhi and Martin Luther King Jr. were all spiritual leaders of nonviolent resistance, yet all three died violent deaths. If these paragons weren't "self-actualized," then who is? Did they suck at creating their realities?

As the central tenet of the New Age movement, YCYOR has come to be associated with a panoply of scams, of varying degrees of nefariousness, from "protective" medallions to cheeseball Ponzi operations. Although the practice of self-responsibility is indisputably constructive, misinterpretations of YCYOR can lead to folly — or worse, judgment worthy of the most rabid fundamentalism.

That said, it is so extraordinary that a popular film has managed to elicit mass interest in existential issues and in the science that can help us to understand them, I, for one, can forgive the filmmakers' subscription a worn-out, New Age half-truth.

SETH SPEAKS

What is the origin of the YCYOR paradigm? The book that probably started it all was *The Nature of Personal Reality* by Jane Roberts. Originally published in 1974, it was the second of several compelling books in which Roberts "channeled" the wisdom of a discarnate entity calling himself Seth. The ground breaking Seth series essentially launched the entire literary genre of channeled books — and, some would say, the New Age movement itself. It may contain the first detailed exposition of the YCYOR concept:

> You create your reality according to your beliefs and expectations, therefore you should examine these carefully. If you do not like some aspect of your world, then examine your own expectations.

> Realize that your physical experience and environment is the materialization of your beliefs. If you find great exuberance, health, effective work, abundance, smiles on the faces of those who you meet, then take it for granted that your beliefs are beneficial. If you see a world that is good, people like you, take it for granted again, that your beliefs are beneficial. But if you find poor health, a lack of meaningful work, a lack of abundance, a world of sorrow and evil, then assume your beliefs are faulty and begin examining them.

> Your world is formed in faithful replica of your own thoughts...If you think positive suggestions to yourself about a situation you send telepathic ammunition for positive use. You must learn to

erase a negative thought or picture by replacing it with its opposite.

You form your own reality. But in forming that reality, you change other realities of which you do not know. The joy, the challenge, the responsibility, the creativity is yours. There is no other message that I can ever give you, or that you can give yourself. You are, each of you, All-That-Is experienced through your own individuality, and the transubstantiation of your flesh.[3]

DOES QUANTUM PHYSICS SUPPORT YCYOR?

What does quantum physics have to say about the idea that "You Create Your Own Reality" and where do some of the other physicists interviewed in *What The Bleep Do We Know!?* stand? More importantly, do we really create our own reality? Is magick real?

As we have already seen, David Albert is publicly dismayed about how his statements contradicting the YCYOR credo were left on the cutting room floor: "The film is pushing a claim that quantum mechanics shows that consciousness is the basis of external reality and that's not an accurate representation."[4]

So, where do Will Arntz and others get the idea that quantum mechanics shows that "You Create Your Own Reality"? David Albert's views are fairly mainstream but they do not reflect the views of all physicists. The idea that YCYOR is supported by quantum physics comes from one of its fundamental precepts:

According to the quantum doctrine, when we make a measurement or perform an observation, we force the myriad possibilities to ante up, snap out of the haze and settle on a single outcome. But between observations — when we are not looking — reality consists entirely of jostling possibilities... The reality of common perception is thus merely a definitive-looking veneer obscuring the internal workings of a highly uncertain cosmos.[5]

Many theoretical physicists extrapolate the observations of subatomic phenomena to a macroscopic scale, positing that the action of our observing the environment causes the surrounding superposition of probabilities to "solidify" into what we perceive as reality. Now, it is one thing to say that observation causes subatomic particles to snap into place and quite another to say that we, observers "create" entire universes with our every thought and every glance; yet this is precisely what the prevailing Many Worlds Interpretation of Quantum Mechanics can be seen to suggest. Pop star physicist, Fred Alan Wolf claims that the application of quantum equations to macro-reality has become a de facto procedure:

> Until very recent times, it was believed that quantum physics only applied to the atomic and subatomic world, a world that was well below human perception. Today, scientists believe that quantum physical effects can also be observed on a larger time and space scale, well within the world of human perception...much as statistical laws are the basis for constructing actuarial tables, quantum physics laws let us calculate very accurately the probabilities for events to occur, even while they remain completely in the dark about the actual events themselves.[6]

Therefore, Will Arntz is *not* smoking angel dust; some physicists do support versions of YCYOR as an interpretation of quantum physics — and others hotly debate it. When I asked my secret prominent physicist to comment on the accuracy of the Fred Alan Wolf quote above, he replied:

> Only partly accurate. Notice that the term "event" implies two characteristics: time and place (perhaps place of a pointer on an apparatus scale). Quantum mechanics does not allow us to calculate "time of events." This is a big scandal — but physicists do not like to discuss it openly, with few exceptions — see for instance [the paper] "Time and Events."[7]

> Concerning the "placing of events" — the statement is also only partly correct. Usually in quantum theory it is assumed that it is impossible to measure simultaneously two or more of "non-commeasurable" observables (like momentum and position pair, Heisenberg uncertainty principle). But this is wrong. See "Simultaneous Measurement of Non-commuting Observables and Quantum Fractals on Complex Projective Spaces."[8]

While hard-bitten materialists angrily maintain that the freakier quantum effects do not apply to the macroscopic scale of matter, "airhead" idealists say that it is the unproven materialist assumptions that need to get chucked…In any case, quantum mechanics complements the "You Create Your Own Reality" adage quite nicely, which is one reason why purveyors of New Age-style products have sought to legitimize and to market themselves by invoking this highfalutin' science.

WHY NEW AGE RHYMES WITH SEWAGE

Here is where the snake oil comes in: The different meanings contained within the terms "you," the "self" and/or the "observer" have been lumped together, leading to a popular misconception that "conscious creation" is performed *solely by the ego*. In most physical theory, in monotheistic religions, as well as in some New Age modalities, there is no distinction made between 1) the ego, 2) the unconscious and 3) the superconscious (a.k.a. "God"). All three aspects are conflated into singular terms such as "you," the "self" and the "observer," though these aspects (which are each further articulated into more levels by various mystical traditions) have distinct attributes.

The conflation of these aspects has its origin in the materialism of Western culture and its offshoot, modern science, where "God" and therefore, superconsciousness do not exist. YCYOR thus evolved into the all-purpose widget, target-marketed to the hapless seeker of the easy answer; thus the New Age movement devolved into the McDonald's of Enlightenment.

The workings of the most complex subjects imaginable i.e., "reality" and "life" were reduced to the catchy one-liner, "You Create Your Own Reality" and transmogrified into a sales pitch for manifold multi-level marketing scams, meditation tapes, assorted cure-alls for diverse materialistic complaints — with not surprisingly — karmic results. The subtext of YCYOR was essentially the same as that of all advertising: "You Suck!"

Another former [Ramtha] student…spent hours

every day following the school's disciplines —
focused breathing, meditation, and concentrating
on a list of positive thoughts, such as I am
fabulously wealthy, I am radiantly healthy, I am
20 years younger, I never age. She believed that
she could heal her own illnesses by generating
a high-frequency force field where decay could
not survive. If she got sick, she thought it was
because she wasn't disciplined enough.

Then, one day, she developed a toothache. She
went to the dentist for the first time in 10 years
and had to get two teeth extracted. "That was my
first indication that something was wrong," she
says. "I did the disciplines every day for years.
But it didn't work. I thought, "I did not maintain
my teeth. I did not reverse aging.'"[9]

"BOOMERITIS"

In the waggish observation of American philosopher
Ken Wilber, the YCYOR paradigm is a classic case of
"boomeritis":

'You create your own reality' — your own
omnipotent ego creates reality — is the absolute
essence of boomeritis…Put simply: boomeritis
is high pluralism mixed with low narcissism.
And that is the strange, strange brew that has
accompanied the Me generation at virtually
every twist and turn of its otherwise idealistic
saga. And with this understanding, my dear
friends, we have arrived at the very heart of this
generation.

The core of New Age spirituality…is the belief

"you create your own reality"…There are, of course, limits to what my beliefs can accomplish. Except if I have boomeritis, in which case the grandiosity involved recognizes no such limitations at all. "Thoughts influence reality" becomes "Thoughts create reality." In order to bolster the notion that my egoic thoughts govern all of reality, it would help if I could claim the authority of the world's great spiritual traditions, if I could claim, that is, the voice of God himself…

Step by step, that is a narcissistic perversion of the mystical view…It is indeed true that the world's great…spiritual traditions maintain that the deepest part of your awareness is one with Spirit, and that this divine oneness can be realized with enlightenment — satori, moksha, cosmic consciousness, unio mystica, call it what you will. I believe that this is the essential truth that many New-Agers are attempting to embrace, and we can all honor that truth, I hope. But the Self that is one with Spirit has little to do with you; it is, in fact, the transcendence of your ego that allows the Spirit to shine forth. **That self is the absolute opposite of boomeritis!**[10]

Wilber goes on to say that "boomeritis" has infected untold academic studies and even modern physics. One cannot help but wonder if boomeritis might have partially motivated university projects, like the Princeton Engineering Anomalies Research Scientific Studies of Consciousness-Related Physical Phenomena, which since 1979 has gathered "clear evidence of an active role of consciousness in the establishment of reality…"[11]

More than 1000 experimental series, employing four different categories of random devices and several distinctive protocols, show comparable magnitudes of anomalous mean shifts from chance expectation, with similar distribution structures. Although the absolute effect sizes are quite small, of the order of 10^{-4} bits deviation per bit processed, over the huge databases accumulated the composite effect exceeds 7σ ($p \approx 3.5 \times 10^{-13}$).[12]

All kidding aside, the PEAR findings consistently show that although consciousness registers very small effects upon random generating devices, the **recurrence** of these small effects is very high.

IS MIND OVER MATTER REAL?

The short answer is yes. There have been thousands of different experiments conducted over the years which show this to be the case, albeit on a rather underwhelming and small scale, such as "10^{-4} bits deviation per bit processed," as noted in the Princeton studies above, and changing of the pH of water "by one full pH-unit," in clinical trials conducted by Stanford University Professor Emeritus physicist, William Tiller, Ph.D., who was also interviewed in *What The Bleep Do We Know!?* Tiller's interesting experiments are discussed in Chapter 10.

On a theoretical level, physicist Fred Alan Wolf speculates that the function of mind is one of converting what he calls *possibility*-waves (sub-units of superpositions) into probability-curves, which in turn produce probabilistic outcomes in the real world. So, in Wolf's view, you unquestionably DO create your own reality, albeit somewhat involuntarily, though he does suggest that people can learn to increase the effect of their will on reality through the practice of meditation and yoga.

The stance of the Penrose-Hameroff model is similar but rather than saying that mind *does* something to the superposition of probabilities, they say that *consciousness* **is the same thing as** *the reduction* of this superposition of probabilities into a single event; that consciousness/self-collapse is itself the non-causal "result" of an objective quantum gravity threshold having been reached by interacting probabilities. **In other words, consciousness does not** *cause* **an event; it is a** *gravitational aspect* **of an event**. This view is rather mechanistic and does not seem to address the self, at all. But hey — maybe they're right...

IS MAGICK REAL?

Wait — didn't we say that quantum physics supports YCYOR? And didn't all these controlled studies prove that human intention affects physical reality? Wouldn't this imply that magick is real? If Wolf and Goswami are right, the answer is maybe — though neither of them addresses the subject of magick in their latest books.

In describing what he calls "mind yoga," Wolf coyly proposes that you can learn how to "focus" on a parallel universe, where the object of your desire is already a fact and potentially increase the likelihood of its manifesting in the universe from which you are sending your "offer" wave...

Wolf also mentions *vibhutis* (also known as *siddhis*), which is Sanskrit for the superhuman abilities of omniscience, telekinesis, levitation, manifesting objects out of thin air, etc. that are reported of fully-realized yogis who, through years of practice have become one with Brahman/Atman ("God").

Where magick implies the manifestation of the ego's desires, a yogi is said to have attained his powers by totally dissolving his or her ego and completely detaching from any earthly desire. The yoga adept has merged with the infinite knowing and creative power of All That Is — and doesn't give a fig about getting stuff through magick, despite having the ability to do so...

DOES CONSCIOUSNESS CREATE THE MATERIAL WORLD?

David Albert says no but according to Fred Alan Wolf and Amit Goswami, the answer is yes. The latter two say basically the same thing, though the way they articulate how this occurs is somewhat different. Wolf implies that humans involuntarily construct their reality around them, during the normal everyday activity of focusing their awareness, for which he uses the technical term, "squaring":

> The mind has the facility to form the "out there" material world of space and time. I am referring here to the operation of "squaring" — the multiplying of one *possibility*-wave by its complex conjugate *possibility*-wave. By this squaring mechanism, objective realities (probability-curves) are created "out there" from the possibility waves undulating within the subjective-unconscious-imaginal sub-spacetime "in-here" realm. In the process of squaring and then dealing with probability-curves, the mind moves from the purely imaginal realm into awareness of the physical realm.

How does the mind construct reality? I speculate that it is by accessing the squaring operation, which is what I believe yoga and other mental disciplines show us how to do. There are two processes involved in the squaring operation. "Squaring," which is the act of bringing the mind into a focus, and "unsquaring," which allows the mind to defocus or "let go" of whatever it has been focused on.[13]

Goswami suggests that the divine Self, peeking out from the awareness of beings in physicality, is what creates the material world:

> …**our consciousness is the consciousness of the being that is beyond the subject-object split**. There is no other source of consciousness in the universe. **The self of self-reference and the consciousness of the original consciousness, together, make what we call self-consciousness**.[14]

> An omnipresent God collapsing the wave function does not resolve the measurement paradox…At what point is the measurement complete if God is always looking? The answer is crucial: **The measurement is not complete without the inclusion of immanent awareness. The most familiar example of an immanent awareness is, of course, that of a human being's brain-mind**.

> **When is the measurement complete? When the transcendent consciousness collapses**

the wave function by means of an immanent brain-mind looking on with awareness. This formulation agrees with our commonsense observation that there is never an experience of a material object without a concomitant mental object, such as the thought I see this object, or without, at least, awareness.[15]

Although, in the film, Goswami is seemingly constructed to be propounding an egocentric, boomeritis version of "You Create Your Own Reality," a full reading of his book, *The Self-Aware Universe: How Consciousness Creates the Material World*, reveals that his view corresponds with the ancient mystical view, which is, your ego does not create reality. Your ego *and* your unconscious, *in conjunction* with the ultimate "Creator" residing within you, who is the universe and of which you are a part, are jointly co-creating reality on myriad levels. In other words, you DO create your own reality — except that "you" aren't only your ego.

SUPERCONSCIOUSNESS VS. SUBURBIA

What is difficult for the Boomer (or anyone) to accept is that the creations of "Your" unconscious and/or spiritual aspects may not be in agreement with the wants of your ego, no matter how intent your ego may be. One of the cruelest interpretations of YCYOR is when people who are seriously ill are blamed for their disease:

> ...illness demonstrates that you are not a good, loving person. The worse the illness, the more unspeakably horrible you have been. Because the ego creates all reality, then a bad ego — an unloving, unkind ego — creates all illness. ...This painfully guilt-inducing claim — you have created your illness — actually benefits

only one group: those selling the books making the claims, who happen — for the moment — to be healthy people who generate a great deal of money and power by telling sick people how to think. As for those who are actually sick, this notion simply acts to instill in them an enormous amount of 'New Age guilt,' which, if anything, will further depress their immune systems and help to make them even sicker.[16]

This kind of judgment is essentially no different from the fundamentalist Christian views that drove Will Arntz away from organized religion:

> ...I was sitting in Sunday school and they were saying that there was only one way to heaven and it was through our lord and savior Jesus Christ. And that if you didn't believe in him, if your Original Sin was not forgiven, then you were going to Hell to burn for all eternity. So I stuck my little hand up and asked, "So a little kid that is born and lives for two years and dies of some disease or accident is going to Hell?" And they said, "Yes." And it was at that moment that I threw a switch. I knew it was all bullshit.[17]

Did the Asian tsunami victims "create" the "reality" of that natural cataclysm? Have the millions of babies born with AIDS worldwide created their reality? Presumably, their egos did not — but if one accepts the idea of karma and the idea of choosing one's incarnations in order to have certain experiences, the answer is yes. There is also the idea that not every rape/war/coalmine collapse victim "causes" their horrible experience; the idea that each soul is a global microcosm of total potential, whereby some experiences may be "attracted" to someone, due to the vacuum created by their sheer lack of any such experiences. This would be the very opposite of "creating reality," in the egotistical sense of "intending" or "manifesting" what one wants to happen.

Is an affluent person, living in a cushy gated community in Sedona superior at "manifesting" the infinite creative potential of the universe than a slum dweller in Kinshasa? When "spirituality" gets confused with wishful thinking, combined with Middle American materialistic values and judgments, we have a problem...

PEAK OIL AND THE END OF SUBURBIA

According to many observers[18], the world's oil production has peaked and no significant new fields have been found in years, while demand is only increasing. Author James Howard Kunstler, who at 56 has doubtless experienced boomeritis directly, says America is in for a long, drawn-out paradigm-shifting tsunami of its own, when the petroleum, upon which every aspect of our civilization is hinged — is gone. He discusses his dire vision of a post-peak oil world in his book, The Long Emergency. In his phlegmatic view, the "You Create Your Own Reality" model, which he dubs the "Jiminy Cricket syndrome" was a byproduct of the cheap fuel available during the 20th Century — which is now drying up:

> **There are at least two major mental disturbances in the collective American mind these days that can be described with some precision. One is the Jiminy Cricket syndrome — the idea that when you wish upon a star your dreams come true [a.k.a. YCYOR]. This is largely a product of the technological**

achievements of the last century, which were themselves a product of cheap energy: namely, things like our trip to the moon, combined with the effects of advertising, Hollywood and pop culture.

We have now become a people who believe that wishing for things makes them happen. Unfortunately, the world just doesn't work that way. The truth is that no combination of alternative fuels or so-called renewables will allow us to run the USA — or even a substantial fraction of it — the way that we're running it now.

There's another mental disturbance that Americans are suffering from. It's the idea that it's possible to get something for nothing — unearned riches, free energy, perpetual motion — and it's exemplified by Las Vegas. Combine the Jiminy Cricket syndrome and the idea that it's possible to get something for nothing and you end up with a population that's thoroughly deluded and unable to deal with reality. That's precisely where we're at.[19]

Our reality-creating skills will surely come in handier than ever, when the oil runs out…

SERENITY

Speaking of the planetary petroleum addiction, the collapse of Western Civilization and the drunken grandiosity of the YCYOR paradigm, the Alcoholics Anonymous *Serenity Prayer* is a sobering antidote: "… grant me the serenity to accept the things I cannot change; courage to change the things I can; and wisdom to know the difference."

CHAPTER 9
DR. MASARU EMOTO &
THE HIDDEN MESSAGES IN WATER

"It was the most beautiful and delicate crystal that I have so far seen — formed by being exposed to the words 'love and gratitude'...I can say that it actually changed my life from that moment on."

Dr. Masaru Emoto
Author of *The Hidden Messages in Water*

THE ART OF WATER

The success of Dr. Masaru Emoto's books both within and outside of Japan has been phenomenal, selling almost half a million copies so far. Many have found his tender haiku-like pronouncements — and his stunning photographs of water crystals — to be quite moving and uplifting.

> I particularly remember one photograph. It was the most beautiful and delicate crystal that I have so far seen — formed by being exposed to the words "love and gratitude." **It was as if the water had rejoiced and celebrated by creating a flower in bloom**. It was so beautiful that I can say that it actually changed my life from that moment on.
>
> **Water had taught me the delicacy of the human soul and the impact that "love and gratitude" can have on the world.**[1]

The ecstasy of Emoto's prose is reminiscent of that found in The Art of Peace by Morihei Ueshiba, founder of Aikido, the Japanese school of martial arts. Shintoist nature worship and a sense of Buddhist nirvana are very much in evidence in the enraptured writings of both men.

> After defeating a high-ranking swordsman (Ueshiba was unarmed), he went into his garden. "Suddenly the earth trembled. Golden vapor welled up from the ground and engulfed me. I felt transformed into a golden image, and my body seemed as light as a feather. All at once I understood the nature of creation: the Way of a Warrior is to manifest Divine Love, a spirit that embraces and nurtures all things. Tears of gratitude and joy streamed down my cheeks. I saw the entire earth as my home, and the sun, moon, and stars as my intimate friends. All attachment to material things vanished."[2]

Emoto developed a technique using a powerful dark field microscope attached with a high-speed camera to photograph newly formed crystals in samples of frozen water, resulting in photographs of mesmerizing beauty.

> …crystals formed in frozen water reveal changes when specific, concentrated thoughts are directed toward them. He found that water from clear springs and water that has been exposed to loving words shows brilliant, complex, and colorful snowflake patterns. In contrast, polluted water, or water exposed to negative thoughts, forms incomplete, asymmetrical patterns with dull colors.[3]

But if you are looking for hard science, Masaru Emoto's latest book, *The Hidden Messages in Water* is not for you. As he states in the bio on his website, "I undertook research of water around the planet not so much as a scientific researcher but as an original thinker, as a human being."[14]

The science in Emoto's previous book, *The Message from Water* was solid enough, however, to garner the attention of Stanford University Professor Emeritus of Material Science and Engineering, William Tiller, Ph.D:

> **Ice Crystal Patterns Materialize Specific Intentions in Water:** In his recent book, "The Message From Water", Masaru Emoto has shown that, **under what appeared to be well controlled conditions**, ice crystal formation in water appears to display relatively unique patterns dependent, not only on the chemical toxicity of various lakes, springs, glaciers and cities where water is collected which is to be expected, but also upon (1) specific music played in a precise environment, (2) wrapping printed statements of appreciation, thanks, anger, hate, etc. on jars of this water for a given time, (3) specific subtle energies, (chi, hado) expressed in the water environment and (4) specific essence additions to water. In all of these examples, it is difficult to evaluate the proportion of the effect on ice crystal pattern formation that comes directly from the physical factors involved and the portion that comes indirectly from the held intentions of the humans involved in the process. It is our belief that a meaningful portion of these beautiful ice crystal patterns arise indirectly from the latter…[5]

THE MEMORY OF WATER

Emoto's work is based on the fascinating principles of homeopathy, whereby successive dilutions of antigens shaken in water produce harmonics and sub-harmonics of the chemicals' molecular patterns. These dilutions are then used to make remedies that stimulate the immune response of patients, without actually exposing them to toxins of any kind, whether they be antigens or pharmaceuticals.

Despite the fact that its effects have been exhaustively proven in countless laboratory studies, homeopathy remains one of the great bugaboos of so-called skeptics worldwide. The American Heritage Dictionary defines a skeptic as "One who instinctively or habitually doubts, questions, or disagrees with assertions or generally accepted conclusions," but more often than not, self-described skeptics are staunch defenders of the prevailing materialist realism of the scientific orthodoxy — and woe to anyone who crosses them.

In her book, *The Field: The Quest for the Secret Force of the Universe*, Lynne McTaggart tells the cautionary tale of allergy specialist, Dr. Jacques Benveniste, head of the French National Institute for Health and Medical Research (INSERM) and whose lab technician accidentally stumbled onto the basic principle of homeopathy in 1984.

Due to an error in calculation, a solution had been diluted to the point where very few of the antigen molecules remained. However, the white blood cells were reacting as if they were being attacked by a high concentration of antigens. After intentionally repeating the dilution mistake and getting the same results, another doctor at the lab, who also happened to be a homeopath, remarked that these experiments were illustrating the fundaments of homeopathy. At the time, Benveniste didn't even know what homeopathy was but he asked the lab technician to dilute the solutions even more, to the point where none of the original active substance would remain.

> In these new studies, no matter how dilute the solution, which was, by now, just plain water, Elisabeth kept getting consistent results, as if the active ingredient was still there...

> The most unexpected phenomenon was yet to come. Although the potency of the anti-IgE was at its highest at concentrations of one part n 1000 (the third decimal solution) and then started to decrease with each successive dilution, as you might logically expect, the experiment took a U-turn at the ninth dilution. The effect of the dilute IgE began increasing at this point and continued to increase, the more it was diluted. As homeopathy had always claimed, the weaker the solution, the more powerful its effect.[6]

Benveniste's findings were replicated in laboratories in France, Israel, Italy and Canada and all thirteen scientists jointly published the findings of their four year study in a 1988 edition of the prestigious and conservative British journal, *Nature*. The popular press jumped all over the story as a validation of homeopathy and declared that Benveniste had discovered the "memory of water," though he already understood that these results had repercussions far beyond any theory of alternative medicine.

> If water were able to imprint and store information from molecules, this would have

an impact on our understanding of molecules and the way they "talk" to one another in our bodies…In any living cell, there are ten thousand molecules of water for each molecule of protein.[7]

DON'T MESS WITH SKEPTICS

Nature was aware of the implications of these findings for the accepted laws of biochemistry, so they agreed to publish the article only after taking the extraordinary step of placing an editorial addendum at the bottom of the article, inviting readers to pick holes in the study. Four days after publication, *Nature* Editor John Maddox showed up at Benveniste's lab with "quackbuster" Walter Stewart and professional magician/debunker-at-large, "The Amazing Randi." Under their supervision, Benveniste's team performed four experiments, one blinded, all of which were successful. Despite the fact that none of the three skeptics were trained in chemistry, Maddox and his team disputed the findings and decided to change the experimental protocol.

Under their new protocol, and amid a charged atmosphere implying that the INSERM team was hiding something, three more tests were done and shown not to work. At this point, Maddox and his team had their results and promptly left… Soon after their five-day visit, *Nature* published a report entitled "High Dilution Experiments a Delusion." It claimed that Benveniste's lab had not observed good scientific protocol. It discounted supporting data from other labs…*Nature*'s results had a devastating effect upon Benveniste's reputation and his position at INSERM…"[8]

Benveniste's career was basically destroyed over the controversy though he was somewhat vindicated thirteen years later, in 2001, when four outside labs, in a series of double-blind experiments overseen by skeptical chemist Madeleine Ennis, reproduced the same phenomenon that he had reported. He has doggedly continued his search for a mechanism by which to explain these results and his laboratory work has shown that water apparently retains the memory of the electromagnetic vibration specific to a chemical.

THE EMAIL MESSAGE OF WATER

In his latest pursuit of digital biology,[9] Benveniste recorded the audio "signature frequencies" of antigens (which are inaudible to the human ear, in a range below 20Hz) and played back these audio samples to water samples, processing the water with the same shaking method of homeopathy, then exposed biological systems ordinarily sensitive to the original antigens to the processed water. In every instance, the biological system was fooled into thinking it has been interacting with the substance, itself. He even emailed audio-MPEG files of these frequencies, producing laboratory results on guinea pig hearts, which showed that "The effects from the digitized water were identical to effects produced on the heart by the actual substances themselves."[10] Jacques Benveniste passed away in October 2004.

CHAPTER 10
WILLIAM TILLER & *CONSCIOUS ACTS OF CREATION*

"It is my belief that our purpose here is to develop our gifts of intentionality and to learn how to be effective creators."

William Tiller, Ph.D.
Professor Emeritus of Material Science and Engineering,
Stanford University
Author of 250 scientific publications and several books,
including *Conscious Acts of Creation* and *Human Transformation*

MIND POWER

In *Conscious Acts of Creation*, William Tiller, Ph.D. trumpets the claim:

> This book marks a sharp dividing line between old ways of scientific thought and old experimental protocols, **wherein, human qualities of consciousness, intention, emotion, mind and spirit cannot significantly affect physical reality**, and a new paradigm wherein they can robustly do so![1]

He is referring to the series of experiments he conducted, by himself and with his associates, Walter Dibble and Michael Kohane, that are the subject of his latest book. Together, they devised a protocol, whereby specific intentions were "imprinted" into simple electrical devices, which they called an IIED (Intention Imprinted Electrical Device). The IIEDs were 7" X 3" X 1" in size and, in order for the experiments to be easily-reproducible by any other interested scientists, the devices were essentially replicas of a commercially available model called the "Ally," made by Clarus Products International. The IIEDs were simple devices, consisting of an Electrically Erasable Programmable Read-Only Memory and an oscillator component (in some experiments, the devices contained three oscillators).

The IIEDs were "imprinted" by placing them on a table, while plugged in and turned on. Four people were seated around the device (all of whom were "accomplished meditators"). First, the meditators mentally "cleansed" the environment and "created a space" for the intention, then they mentally "erased" any prior intentions from the device, then they focused on a prearranged statement, which related to the target of the experiment, and finally their closing intention was to "seal" the imprint into the device and minimize any leakage of their intention. The devices were then stored in a Faraday Cage (a sealed container made of a conducting material which acts as an electromagnetic shield) until they were shipped to another lab, 2,000 miles away, and upon arrival they were stored in a Faraday cage until their use in the experiments conducted by other scientists.

During the experiments, these devices were placed three to six inches from the various targets and were shown to significantly influence these, simply by putting the devices close to them and turning them on. The effects were tested on both inanimate and animate systems (i.e., water and fruit fly larvae), and it was repeatedly shown that "the human quality of **focused intention** can be made to act as a true thermodynamic potential and strongly influence experimental measurements for a variety of specific target experiments. In addition, continued use of this protocol in a given experimental locale leads to a unique conditioning of that space."[2]

SUMMARY OF "IIED" EXPERIMENTS & RESULTS
1) WATER STUDIES

> **Intention:** To raise or decrease the pH of water by one pH unit, i.e.. increase or decrease the H+ content of this water by a factor of 10.
>
> **Result: Up to 1 pH unit increase and decrease of water samples was achieved.**

2) IN VIVO FRUIT FLY STUDIES

> **Intention:** To influence the availability of nutrients and enzymes in fruit fly larvae, resulting in significantly reduced development time, relative to that of an unimprinted control device.
>
> **Result: 15% reduction in larval development time for those exposed to imprinted device vs. the control group of larvae.**

3) IN VITRO ENZYME STUDIES

> **Intention:** To influence a device so as to increase the thermodynamic activity of a liver enzyme, alkaline phosphatase.
>
> **Result: 10-20% increases in the thermodynamic activity of ALP of those samples exposed to imprinted device vs. the control group exposed to unimprinted device.**

4) LOCALE CONDITIONING STUDIES

Intention: To influence a device so as to make it a powerful locale conditioning system, such that any subsequent IIED or psychoenergetic experiment conducted in that conditioned locale is to be successful to a high degree.

Result: Unusually large oscillations in water temperature, pH, electrical conductivity and DC magnetic field polarity effects indicated that the conditioning of the locale "and the second phase of the new physics development was undeniably achieved."

The conclusion reached by Tiller, Dibble and Kohane:

> …under at least some conditions, human intention acts like a typical potential capable of creating robust effects in what we call physical reality. This significantly broadens the purview of physics, challenges its present perspectives, mindsets and laws, and sets it on a new course toward understanding how physical matter and energy are connected to human consciousness.[3]

WHY ARE HUMANS SO LAME AT TELEKINESIS?

During the 1970s, there was a recurring theme in science fiction movies, exemplified by such films as *Scanners* and *The Fury*, which depicted government laboratories churning out these seemingly innocuous persons — who actually had the ability to levitate the bodies and explode the heads of their adversaries! Though Tiller describes the results of his IIED experiments as "robust," his results are not exactly the controlled telekinesis of large objects that one would hope for...

It seemed pretty remarkable to me that electronic devices which had been "imprinted" with specific intentions by a small group of four meditators and which were then FedExed to a lab two thousand miles away had managed to produce consistent, measurable (if small) effects on water samples, fruit fly larvae and pig kidney enzymes when they were placed within three to six inches from these target groups, as compared with control groups, which were exposed to the unimprinted devices. Nevertheless, "Conscious Acts of Creation" are not *quite* the words I would use to describe the 10-20% "statistically significant" increases in the thermodynamic activity of the enzyme, alkaline phosphatase, derived from pig kidneys...

The prominent physicist, whom I consulted on the matter and who wishes to remain anonymous, had this to say when I asked to comment on Tiller's Conscious Acts of Creation experiments:

> It consists of two, largely disjointed, parts: experimental and theoretical. The experimental part is negligible in consequences. Small changes of physicochemical properties of water etc. can be attributed to many factors — they cannot convince scientists that something "strange" is going on — **except of strange experimental protocols** [Emphasis added].
>
> The theoretical part has nothing whatsoever to do with the experimental part, except that adding a "theoretical explanation" that no one understands adds to the unintelligibility of the book...

Even Tiller admits that the effect of human intention on physical reality is kind of lame and not so "robust," after all; he suggests that this is possibly due to evolutionary causes:

> One hypothesis is that the effect of our intention on physical reality is limited as a result of natural selection as well. The capacity to do real harm to each other could be significantly enhanced by human intentions manifesting robustly. This concept would tend to justify thinking that human intention can only produce small, barely perceptible effects on physical reality.

But Tiller goes on to suggest that our telekinetic abilities might be enhanced if we replace our current view:

> Such a viewpoint needs to be replaced by one that is a bit more expansive; namely, that development of sufficient inner self-management [i.e. meditation] allows one to circumvent these limitations without serious side effects.[4]

Tiller says lots of things that one would not expect of a physicist with tenure at such an august institution as Stanford University. For example, this quote from **What The Bleep Do We Know!?**: "All of us, one day will reach the level of avatars who we have read about in history, the Buddhas, the Jesus."

THE TILLER MODEL

The main thrust of Tiller's recent work has been to map out the physics of the soul, as it interfaces with physical reality.

Biobodysuit Metaphor

- Each layer has unique substance and infrastructure
- The outer 2 layers constitute temporal physical reality
- The middle shell is non-temporal and could be called the soul
- The layer infrastructure and the coupling between layers largely determine the state of the Wellness of the Whole Person[5]

The biobodysuits are fabricated with four unique layers, (1) the outermost layer is fashioned from electric monopole substances (particulate substance), (2) the first inner layer is fashioned from magnetic monopole (de Broglie wave substance), (3) the second inner layer is fashioned from emotion domain substances and (4) the third layer is fashioned from mind domain substances. These three layers are all substructures of the physical vacuum! And inside this biobodysuit is a portion of our spirit self that drives the vehicle...

All of these inner layer substances function in what we presently call "the vacuum" and, the more structurally refined are these layers, the larger is the amount of our high spirit self that can inhabit the biobodysuit. What are known as the four fundamental forces of present-day science all function in the outermost layer and somewhat in the first layer of the biobodysuit. What are presently called "subtle energies" all function in the three inner layers which are substructures of the vacuum.[6]

Tiller hypothesizes that human consciousness is the by-product of "higher dimensional" spiritual energies entering dense matter. He coins the term "deltron," as the "coupling substance" of emotional energy, which has the function of binding what he terms the four dimensions of the physical world with the four dimensions of the subtle or thought world, via the two subspaces that are reciprocals of each other, what he terms "D-space" and "R-space":

> One subspace, which we call direct-space (or D-space), has a distance-time coordinate framework. The other subspace, which we call reciprocal-space (or R-space) has an inverse-distance and inverse-time coordinate framework. The latter coordinates can be looked at as frequencies and thus allow a more natural bridge to the higher dimensional domains of nature (emotion, mind and spirit).

A word picture of the simplest composite substance would be

> {D-Space Substance //Activated Deltrons// R-Space Substance}.

> Since the magnitude of this coupling increases as the magnitude of deltron activation increases, we can conclude that enhanced human intention is or includes a thermodynamic potential to increase deltron activation. We can also conclude that it is not the dense particulate substance of physical reality that gives rise to these new phenomena. Rather, it is the much finer wave substance of physical reality that gives

birth to these new expressions of nature. Thus, we must begin to recognize physical reality as being composed of two parts, a dense electric matter part and a fine magnetic matter part. Only when large deltron (from the emotion domain) activation occurs is this magnetic monopole aspect readily distinguishable from the electric monopole aspect. (Magnetic dipoles manifesting measurable effects in dense physical matter are thought to arise as "images" from the magnetic monopoles in reciprocal-space).

Specific Physical	=	D-space Part + R-space Part
Measurement	=	Local Part + Non-local Part
	=	Particle Part + Wave Part

Most people think of the physical vacuum as totally empty but, actually, it is the space between all atoms and almost all of the space within atoms and molecules (at least 99.999+% of that space). From theory, for internal consistency of quantum mechanics and relativity theory, the vacuum must contain $\sim 10^{94}$ grams equivalent of latent energy ($E = mc^2$ units). This is a huge number which, in more practical terms, means that the amount of vacuum energy latent in the volume of a single hydrogen atom is much, much more than all of the mass energy present in all of the planets and all of the stars that telescopes would detect in a radius of 20 billion light years (provided that we can neglect the Einsteinian gravitational constant — which one can if we have a "flat" universe — and cosmological data suggest that we do).[7]

Tiller's ideas are certainly intriguing, suggesting a mathematical and completely scientific explication of the soul, consciousness and the interplay between the subtle and gross physical realms. It is especially interesting that Tiller's experimenters recorded and documented the residual effects of consciousness on a location used in numerous experiments, whereby the effects of the "imprinting" continued to resonate in the space and affect the subsequent experiments.

All of Tiller's statements above are supported by what seemed to me to be reams and reams of math, which, as a total math-o-phobe, I am not capable of evaluating. My anonymous prominent physicist consultant has the following to say about Tiller's math in *Conscious Acts of Creation*: "All the math in the book is either trivial (that is, on a student level and has nothing to do whatsoever with the subject matter) or else — nonsensical."

I forgot to ask my cranky friend if he would like some *deltrons* with that shake! He posted further lengthy comments about Tiller's model and the work of other physicists interviewed in **What The Bleep Do We Know!?** on one of his blogs.[8]

CHAPTER 11
JOHN HAGELIN, PH.D. FOR PRESIDENT

"...perhaps I am best known for the Supersymmetric Flipped SU(5) Grand Unified Field Theory."

John Hagelin, Ph.D.
Professor of Physics and Director of the Institute of
Science, Technology & Public Policy at Maharishi University
Author of *Manual for a Perfect Government*
and *Physiology of Consciousness*

HAGELIN FOR PRESIDENT

Of the many interesting people interviewed in **What The Bleep Do We Know!?**, perhaps one of the most interesting is John Hagelin, Ph.D., who during the film's closing segment, where all the interviewees identify themselves says:

> After my Ph.D. from Harvard, I went to CERN, the European lab for particle research and then joined faculty at Stanford and my work there has been the development of unified quantum field theory. I have about 100 publications in this area but **perhaps I am best known** for the Supersymmetric Flipped SU(5) Grand Unified Field Theory [Emphasis added].

One might think that, rather than work he did on some arcane physics theories, his having been a three-time US presidential candidate could be the thing for which he would be best known (in 1992 and 1996 for the Natural Law Party, founded by Maharishi Mahesh Yogi and in 2000 for the Reform Party founded by Ross Perot).

Hagelin is a gifted speaker, who effortlessly weaves his profound insights about quantum physics with his ideas of public policy and he gets standing ovations from adoring crowds of Transcendental Meditation followers. He is currently lobbying the US government to subsidize his plan for the *Vedic Defense Shield*, a novel means to protect the nation that he boldly claims is a "permanent, proven solution to terrorism tragedies and wars, and [the] creation of lasting world peace."[1] You've got to love the delicious subversion of trying to land a defense contract to pay for a group meditation project — turning Dr. Strangelove on his ear!

The *Shield* would consist of 8,000 meditators, i.e., "one square root of one percent of the planetary population," which is the necessary amount needed to create the shift in mass consciousness to "create world peace" by following the Maharishi way. Detractors claim this would require that each meditator buy over $100,000 worth of Maharishi products. 8,000 multiplied by $100,000 would be a significant chunk of the US Taxpayer's change. Whistleblowers cry foul but I suppose I wouldn't mind seeing Transcendental Meditation™ successfully hustle a piece of the American Pie, up there with Lockheed Martin and Boeing. After all, the US Government daily spends plenty more taxpayer money on programs much more nefarious than the *Vedic Defense Shield*.

Transcendental Meditation™ founder, Maharishi Mahesh Yogi himself graduated from college with a degree in physics and the movement's "Natural Law" is based on Maharishi's melding of ancient Hindu cosmology with modern physical theory, touted as a "Scientific Programme to Create Lasting WORLD PEACE":

Quantum cosmology concludes that there is only one, unified wholeness at the fundamental level of the Unified Field of Natural Law and no real fundamental division into observer and observed. Thus quantum cosmology verifies that the Unified Field observes itself in a completely self-referral [sic] manner and thereby confirms that the unmanifest, quantum-mechanical Unified Field of Natural Law is a field of self-referral consciousness which generates the whole manifest universe by its process of self-observation...

Maharishi's Vedic Science offers complete and systematic knowledge of the eternal self-referral dynamics of the field of pure consciousness knowing itself. It provides the direct subjective approach to the unified basis of Natural Law, the Unified Field of Natural Law, the field of pure consciousness—the field of *Atma*, the Self of every individual.

In Vedic Language, the Unified Field is called Samhita, the observer is called Rishi, process of observation is called Devata, and the observed is called Chhandas... [2]

For all the TM™ movement's claims that their "Vedic Science" creates "increased coherence and harmony," there seems to be some degree of decoherence between Hagelin and his former CERN colleagues. According to *Nature* magazine, Hagelin was asked by the co-authors to stop linking their SU(5) theory with Transcendental Meditation™:

Two-page advertisements, with row after row of partial differential equations, appear regularly in US newspapers describing how the theoretical physics work of Hagelin and others explains the impact of TM on distant events. Hagelin often lectures on $SU(5)$ and other unified field theories to both scientific and nonscientific audiences, mixed in with a lengthy discussion of TM.

Not surprisingly, the linkage of $SU(5)$ with TM infuriates his former collaborators. It is hard enough, they complain, to win scientific support for any type of unified theory. "A lot of people [Hagelin] has collaborated with in the past are very upset about this, " says Jorge Lopez, a Texas A&M University physicist. "It's absolutely ludicrous to say that TM has anything to do with flipped $SU(5)$."

John Ellis, director of CERN's theoretical physics dept., has asked Hagelin to stop mixing TM and $SU(5)$. "I was worried about guilt by association," Ellis explains. "I was afraid that people might regard [Hagelin's assertions] as rather flaky, and that might rub off on the theory or on us."[3]

On Columbia mathematics professor Peter Woit's blog, there are some observations made about Hagelin's former stature in the world of theoretical physics, as an example of the psychological dissociation which can lurk in a field of such rarified abstraction:

Posted by woit at September 27, 2004 07:00 PM:
...His 73 papers are mostly about supersymmetric GUTs and considered quite respectable, with

a total of over 5000 citations, including 641 citations for one of them alone. Hagelin was a grad student at Harvard when I was an undergrad and I met him when we were in the same quantum field theory class…**I remember Hagelin wanting to discuss how quantum field theory could explain how [Transcendental Meditators] were able to levitate, something about how they did this by changing the position of the pole in the propagator. The fact that someone who spouts such utter nonsense can get a Ph.D. from Harvard and be one of the most widely cited authors on supersymmetric models is pretty remarkable.**

Posted by Peter at September 28, 2004 02:20 PM:
…whenever one is dealing with highly speculative ideas that have no connection with experiment, there's a danger of becoming delusional and thinking that you're doing real science when you're not…**I think it's a good idea for people to consider the example of Hagelin: he's completely delusional and has zero common sense, but able to function at a high level in the particle theory community. One should take seriously the danger that he's not the only one deluding himself.**[4]

Hagelin currently holds the titles of Director of the Institute of Science, Technology and Public Policy at Maharishi University of Management[5] and Minister of Science and Technology of the Global Country of World Peace.[6] The latter is another organ of the Maharishi Mahesh Yogi, which recently bought a building in Lower Manhattan for an eight-figure sum and which has its own global currency, issued in the Netherlands. Talk about creating your own reality!

As to Hagelin's US presidential candidacies, former members of the Transcendental Meditation™ movement, who have put together a cult awareness website have this to say:

> What few publications have dared to report is that Hagelin is a "stealth" candidate for the Maharishi Mahesh Yogi's Transcendental Meditation movement — an extreme, fundamentalist Hindu sect with bizarre goals for world domination.[7]

YOGIC HIGH-FLYING

According to these former TM™ members, the Maharishi's Natural Law Party, which has been established in several countries around the world and on whose platform Hagelin ran, aims to replace local laws, such as the US Constitution with the ancient Vedic Laws, Manu Dharma Shastras, which were codified some 2,500 years ago and include the instatement of a caste system. "[The Maharishi] is particularly fond of the caste system, which he feels fosters purity of the races and allows those who follow it a simpler life, with more time for meditation."[8]

These same former members say that TM™ is a predatory fleecing operation, where supplicants are charged $1,200 to receive their own "personal" mantra which they are not to reveal to anyone, although these classical mantras have been in existence for millennia and are available in cheap Penguin Paperbacks. "One former Transcendental Meditation member estimates the true cost of "enlightenment" à la TM™ at over

$162,000 [over the course of several years] — circa the mid-'90s. The Maharishi has increased the cost considerably since then."[9]

These sources say that the reason why the Maharishi group strongly refuses to be classified as a religion is in order to qualify for government subsidies for their government programs, such as instituting TM™ in public schools and the above-mentioned *Vedic Defense Shield*.

In the early 1990s, Pulitzer prize-winning author Michael D'Antonio performed an in-depth study of the New Age movement in America. His views on the movement were positive overall; however, regarding TM™, D'Antonio wrote:

> I would have welcomed the discovery of a middle way, a path to spirituality that was consistent with reason. But TM, as it is practiced at MIU, isn't a middle ground. For the first time in my travels through New Age America, I worried that I was observing a cult rather than a culture. MIU and the Maharishi would take control of everything — right down to matters of food, shelter, and child rearing... [TMers, D'Antonio concludes,] have accepted rigid, authoritarian control in exchange for security. Far from being a place where individuals grow and innovate, the Fairfield TM community is regimented and constricted. All conflict, doubt, perhaps even all genuine emotion, is stifled and covered over with a pleasant veneer.[10]

In fairness, it should be noted, "The reasons that people leave movements are as many as the reasons that initially attract them to a group. Transcendental Meditation™ is not alone among religious movements that promise a scientific pathway to 'bliss,' 'truth,' 'total freedom,' etc."[11] Indeed, many people claim to be grateful for the benefits of Transcendental Meditation™ and over 5 million people have completed the basic course worldwide.

WASHINGTON, D.C. CRIME STUDY

One questionable statement Hagelin makes in the film regards the 1993 Washington, D.C. Transcendental Meditation™ study he was involved in to reduce violent crime in the city that has the distinction of one of the highest per-capita homicide rates in the US. The study, which forms the basis for his *Vedic Defense Shield* plan, was conducted in June and July of 1993, during which time 5,000 people performed Transcendental Meditation™ in Washington, D.C. By their own account, the number of Homicides, Rapes, and Assaults (HRA) was reduced by 18% as a result of their practice of TM™ during that time period:

However, independent and unbiased sources report:

> **Based on the numbers reported in their own study, the HRA crime rate was about 30% higher in 1993 than the average crime rate between 1988-1992.** The HRA crime rate showed a decline around the middle of the two month period where TM was practiced and remained relatively low (by 1993 standards) for several months afterward, though the decline was small enough that the reduced HRA crime rate was still about 10-15% higher than average at that time of year. **There was no reduction in the homicide rate during the period of the study. Whether**

> **this means that TM caused a drop in that year's unusually high HRA rate, or whether the HRA rate naturally dropped closer to its more typical frequency is the issue.**[12]

ISTPP's argument for the "success" of their project was that 1993 was a hotter summer than average. Increased temperatures statistically result in increased violent crimes, therefore: "Analysis of 1993 data, **controlling for temperature**, revealed that there was a highly significant decrease in HRA crimes associated with increases in the size of the group during the Demonstration Project."[13]... Are we creating out own reality yet?

I might be creating my own reality here, but I prefer to think of Hagelin's schtick as highly sophisticated and subversive performance art, a mischievous stand against the insanity of our current political landscape. Whatever is ultimately going on with him, he is certainly better at doing Supersymmetric Flipped Grand Unified Theory equations than 99.99% of us ...

CHAPTER 12
CANDACE PERT, PH.D. &
THE MOLECULES OF EMOTION

"...the body is inseparable from the mind..."

Candace Pert, Ph.D.
Professor of Physiology and Biophysics, Georgetown
University Medical School
Former Section Chief of Brain Biochemistry Clinical Neuroscience
Branch, National Institute of Mental Health (NIMH)
Author of numerous books, including *Psychosomatic Wellness*
and *Molecules of Emotion: the Science Behind Mindbody Medicine*.
Holder of numerous patents for modified peptides.

MOLECULES DO IT

Of all the books reviewed here, Candace Pert, Ph.D.'s
Molecules of Emotion is the easiest read, not because its science
is any less complicated but because it is couched within
a gripping, well-crafted narrative about the triumphs and
the blunders in this woman's notable career, while she
navigated the Byzantine politics of neuroscience.

Because much of Pert's work was an exploration of the
many *receptors*, which cluster along our bodies' cells,
the book begins with a quick primer on the basics of
neurochemistry. The first thing to know is that a *receptor*
is a single protein molecule, which lies in the cellular
membrane of cells located all over the body. There can
be can be up to 70 different kinds of these receptor
molecules on any given cell, 50,000 of one type, 10,000
of another, 100,000 of a third and so on. Receptors
function as sensing molecules; they are the eyes, the ears,

the nose, the mouth and fingers of our cells.

> All receptors are proteins…And they cluster in the cellular membrane waiting for the right chemical keys to swim up to them through the extracellular fluid and to mount them by fitting into their keyholes — a process known as binding.

Binding. It's sex on a molecular level!

> And what is this chemical key that docks onto the receptor and causes it to dance and sway? The responsible element is called a ligand. This is the chemical key that binds the receptor, entering it like a key in a keyhole, creating a disturbance to tickle the molecule into rearranging itself, changing its shape until — click! — information enters the cell.

> Ligands are generally much smaller molecules than the receptors they bind to, and they are divided into three chemical types. The first type of ligand comprises the classical neurotransmitters… these are the smallest, simplest of molecules, generally made by the brain to carry information across the gap, or synapse, between one neuron and the next…A second category of ligands is made up of steroids, which include the sex hormones…My favorite category of ligands by far, and the largest, constituting perhaps 95 percent of them all, are the peptides. As we shall see, these chemicals play a wide role in regulating practically all life processes…**If the cell is the engine that drives all life then the receptors**

**are the buttons on the control panel of that
engine and the specific peptide (or other kind
of ligand) is the finger that pushes the button
and gets things started.**[1]

EUREKA!

Neurotransmitters were only just being discovered and
neuroscience did not even exist as a medical discipline
when Pert enrolled in Johns Hopkins Medical School's
Pharmacology Department, as a married 24-year-old
mother of a small boy. As fate would have it, she landed
herself in a research-based program in a laboratory
where many of these discoveries were being made. Her
professor was Sol Snyder, an extremely ambitious wild-
man, a sort of Mick Jagger of pharmacology. To Snyder,
science was a game, which he took every advantage to
win, with two secretaries churning out grant proposals
and his predatory eye on the lookout for studies that he
could scoop.

He would teach Pert his winning methodologies that she
would later teach to her own students. One of these was
to "trust your hunches." After her several failed trials,
when Sol told her to cease looking for the opiate receptor,
she went behind his back, and using his laboratory's
funds, ordered a batch of radioactive naxolone from a
lab in Boston. She had been unable to find the opiate
receptor using morphine but knew that, as a powerful
opiate antagonist that is used as an antidote for overdose,
naxolone locks into the same receptor as opiates like
heroin and morphine and bumps off and blocks them
from entering the cells of both humans and animals.
By "labeling" naxolone with a radioactive isotope,
and mixing it with a monkey-brain "milkshake" she
hypothesized that would finally get a clear reading:

"Sol, you're not going to believe it!" I exclaimed, laying my open notebook down on the desk.

"It worked! It worked! We've found the opiate receptor!"

Intent and silent, he studied the numbers I had written in the notebook, lingering over them for a full minute while I stood barely breathing by his side.

"Fuck," he said in a low voice, continuing to look at the numbers. I began to feel apprehensive. Was he getting mad because I'd gone ahead and done the experiment against orders?

"Fuck, fuck, fuck!" he began to sputter, and then looked up at me, his face lighting up in a wild grin. He jumped up from his chair and began to pace excitedly around the office.

"The ball's in your court," he turned and announced to me suddenly. "You can have whatever you need. You can have Adele Snowman as your technician. Get her to repeat the experiment, and if it works, you've got her for good!"

...I had made Sol happy! And now, as a reward, he was doing the unthinkable, plucking me out of my lowly status a graduate student and thrusting me into a league light-years beyond...[2]

The experiment was repeated numerous times and within 6 weeks, a 15-paragraph paper was submitted to prestigious *Science* journal and immediately accepted, published in March 1973. Soon Pert was off, lecturing all over the country. Her technique of using radioactive antagonists, along with some other lab tricks she developed with "magic membranes," shaking and filtering soon led to the discovery by Sol's lab of several more receptors, such as the norepinephrine receptor, the GABA receptor and the dopamine receptor. She herself found opiate receptors in snakes, rats, birds and in the gruesomely ugly hagfish. Opiate receptors were eventually found on lowly single-celled creatures and in insects. The competition soon became fierce from other labs, who wanted to score coups based on their findings:

> ...Sol called me into his office one Spring morning in 1973 and told me to contact the Baltimore morgue, pronto. He'd heard that a competitor was planning to publish data from a study of opiate receptors in the human brain and our latest paper, which we had just prepared for *Nature*, contained only monkey-brain data. Sol wanted me to get some human brains, run them through my assay, and quickly assemble some data for the paper before I went off to the journal...When I arrived at the morgue, the pathology clerk sent me into to a room where I saw three naked bodies lying on three separate tables...One, I was told was a man who had dropped dead playing tennis that morning, the other two were a liquor store owner and the young man who had attempted to rob him... My heart was pounding as the pathologist went to work, eventually placing a brain in each of my three ice buckets. I thanked him coolly, as if I saw brains being removed from men's bodies every day.[3]

As Pert waited late into the night for the results of her

hastily prepared experiment, when everyone else had gone home, she became pensive:

> Many times in the laboratory I've felt I was moving close to the mystery, but never more powerfully than when I walked back into the cold room that night and saw the remains of those three human brains — 3-pound universes when alive, in death looking like nothing so much as half-eaten turkey carcasses — waiting to be swept into the garbage. The fragility of life, the ruthlessness of science, the folly and the beauty of it all moved through me, striking an emotional chord so powerful I can still feel its vibration.

> ...I looked at the [newspaper] pictures of this man and then at the numbers in my notebook, wondering how he would react if he knew we'd made a milkshake of his brain. Considering what he'd done to the guy who had tried to rob his store, not too cordially. Even so, I hoped he'd be glad to have helped in the fight against drug addiction.[4]

Two years later, after Pert had moved on to work at the National Institute of Mental Health, a British lab finally isolated the chemical formula for endorphin, the natural opiate produced by the body. The principals involved with that study, along with Sol Snyder, were given the prestigious Lasker Award, considered a stepping-stone to the Nobel Prize for their complementary receptor/endorphin research. Sol had baldly taken credit for Pert's role in the discovery of the receptor! He did, however invite her to be a guest at the ceremony:

This was too bitter a pill to swallow, to have to stand alongside those who had failed to go the nine yards, when I was the one who had done the brain-breaking work to put the cap on the opiate receptor search, and had done it, despite the abandonment of the research by a man who was now accepting the award for it. No, I told myself, I couldn't let it happen, to be forgotten and ignored by history, while the boys waltzed away with the prize.[5]

Pert proceeded to break an unwritten rule within the hallowed halls of science: she made a big stink. Pert wrote to the Lasker's benefactress and to the science media, protesting her exclusion and the story spread from there. In his book *Apprentice to Genius*, Robert Kanigel would later write about how Pert embarrassed a "royal dynasty" of medicine. When Sol and the others were later nominated for the Nobel Prize and the committee asked her to vouch for them, she declined and they did not win the prize. Pert's politically damaging moves would dog her career and contribute towards impeding the acceptance of her future developments, including a potential avenue to cure AIDS.

BAD MEDICINE

Virtually all Americans have experienced some degree of cynicism and resignation in the face of the medical system of the US, or as Pert herself notes:

It's obvious the public is catching on to the fact that they're the ones paying monstrous health care bills for often worthless procedures to remedy conditions that could have been prevented in the first place.[6]

Yet, it is not often that one gets an insider's view of the internecine power struggles that occur on the front lines of medicine. The reader may be shocked at the pettiness and selfishness that governs medical research at every step of the game; starting with the tactics in paper-writing, which can jeopardize the implementation of life-saving treatments:

> [A common strategy]…was to publish at the very end of the year, thereby preventing any particularly facile competitor from seeming to scoop the discovery by publishing his own version in a different journal during the same year. Any subsequent publication would bear a post-1975 date…

> The percentage of papers that get cited more than a few times is very small, and for this reason, everyone always refers to their own previous papers as much as possible. Because appearing in print is so important, and because modern scientific projects can involve several collaborators, **more bitter and more intense arguments arise over the order of authorship on a paper than the thorniest of theoretical issues…**

> [When Pert had been frantically trying to find a cure for her father's lung cancer, enlisting the help of other researchers], The Cancer Institute lab chief was furious at how I'd squandered the hot finding about the growth of cancer cells by releasing it, in his eyes, prematurely. **I'd done the unspeakable, packing our paper with data that any self-respecting scientists would have spun out over three or four papers, thereby**

increasing the number of publications, to say nothing of all the chances to get cited...

Clearly, my ex-collaborator believed I had poached on his turf, and I believed, just as clearly, that **his territorial maneuvering, driven by a self-aggrandizing motive to get as much credit for the research as he could, was the stuff that kept medical science from finding desperately-needed treatments.** My father was dead and I no longer had a shred of a reason to stay in the cancer doctor's good graces.[7]

...to outright theft, as when Watson and Crick stole the work of the actual discoverer of the DNA molecule, Rosalind Franklin:

> ...the two men visited Franklin's lab when she was out of town, persuaded her boss to let them take a peek at her data...they stole Franklin's data and got away clean, tossing her a bone of acknowledgement in their seminal paper, which won them the biggest award in science [The Nobel Prize]. In his best-selling book, Watson actually boasts about the theft...[8]

THE FIGHT TO CURE AIDS

Pert's reputation as a cantankerous feminist was not the only obstacle in her way. The other hurdles were her "heretically cross-disciplinary" approach to science and her own lack of business savvy:

> **My sojourn into the AIDS arena in some ways paralleled my earlier foray into the world of cancer research, when we failed**

> **to convince the narrowly-specialized field that neuroscience had something to offer** in developing treatments for cancer…Huge amounts of money were coming down the pipeline for AIDS research, and to get a piece of the pie, we needed the goodwill of powerful people in high places, something we soon found out we did not have.[9]

During Pert's desperate attempts to save her father's life from lung cancer, she had discovered that there was a connection between small cell cancer, the immune system and toxicity in the body. The gook deposited in the lungs from smoking cigarettes causes the immune system to go into hyper response, sending more and more white blood cells to try to repair the damage. This over-cranked mêlée eventually results in damage to the lung cells' DNA, which grow wildly in response to peptide hormones like bombesin and proceed to metastasize all over the body, following peptide signals.

The data accumulated by Pert and her second husband, Michael Ruff, suggested that the same peptides found in the brain were also found in the immune, nervous and endocrine systems. The peptides appeared to be functionally integrated, in what she called a *psychoimmunoendocrine* network. Their revolutionary discovery appeared in print for the first time in the September 1984 issue of the journal *Science*,[10] spurring the creation of the new field of *psychoneuroimmunology* or PNI (a nomenclature she did not agree with but the name stuck).

Their approach to attacking the HIV virus was novel in terms of virology but it was old hat from the standpoint of neuroscience. They could easily see how viruses might operate like ligands, binding, just like peptides, to specific receptors. Since numerous HIV studies had already proven that the virus enters the body and infects by binding with the T4 receptors on immune cells, they reasoned that if they could find the body's natural peptide ligand that fits the T4 receptor, it could yield a simple, nontoxic therapeutic drug to stop the virus from entering the cell.

The HIV virus looks something like a World War II sea mine; it is a ball with spikes, made up of gp120 molecules. Fragments of the gp120 spikes fall off of the virus' protein envelope and block the immune cell's receptors for vasoactive intestinal peptide (VIP), among others:

> When gp120 binds to receptors in the brain and preempts VIP activity, neurons die or equally as damaging, lose their axons and dendrites, causing the dementia effects observed in an increasing percentage of AIDS patients...The gp120 receptor occupation...shortens the life span of T4 lymphocytes, resulting in an impaired immune system and increased susceptibility to opportunistic disease, the cause of death for most people with AIDS.

> This new understanding was in direct opposition, once again to what most other AIDS researchers believed at the time, which it was that it was the direct infection of the cell by the HIV virus that caused symptoms of AIDS. We saw it more simply, as the blockage of VIP, resulting in a failure of neurons to grow immune cells to mature. (The wasting effects of AIDS — weight loss, failure to thrive — were to be understood much later, using our same theory, when we proved that the

gp120 also fit and blocked the receptor for the growth-stimulating hormone, GHRH.)[11]

Pert and her husband synthesized a peptide to mimic gp120, which they called "Peptide T" and ran some tests, which showed that it competed with the HIV for half of the immune cells' T4 receptors. Just hours later, their friends' lab reported that their peptide was 80-90% effective in preventing the growth of HIV in human cells. "This type of result, showing comparable relative potency in two very different methods, was the old standard for a receptor effect, and it clinched it for us. We knew we really had something."[12]

They encountered great difficulty getting their discoveries published, due to their "heretically interdisciplinary" application of *psychoneuroimmunology* to virology. The reigning worldview in medicine held firmly to the denial of any connection between mind and body as this related to health and disease. The very structure of The National Institute of Health, itself mirrored the old Cartesian split: National Institute of Mental Health, where Pert worked was supposed to research everything above the neck, while the larger, better-funded NIH took care of everything below the neck.

TOXIC WARFARE

The NIH and the Cancer Institute already had their own conventional candidate for an AIDS treatment, a highly toxic drug called AZT. This chemotherapeutic drug, originally used for treatment of cancer in the early sixties works by terminating virus replication. The negative side effect is that it terminates healthy cells, especially immune cells, ultimately undermining the patient's health. As a researcher who had spent her entire life in a laboratory, she was ill-prepared to tangle with the agendas of powerful pharmaceutical corporations:

> Clinical trials involve millions of dollars, the futures of entire companies…the necessity to thread your way through the intricate maze of the FDA, and a political sense that was entirely foreign to [me]…I was completely unprepared to deal with the kind of real-world, big-business wheeling and dealing that was necessary if I was going to have any hope of having a direct impact on people's health.[13]

The final blow came when a Harvard researcher announced at a conference that "Peptide T" was not effective because he and his colleagues at the NIH had failed to replicate their anti-viral effects in vitro. When Pert reviewed his data, she found that these other labs had not accurately followed her steps. She could not help wondering if their "failure-to-replicate" been the result of a simple mistake or if their Cartesian worldview had prevented them from doing an unbiased experiment. There was also the more disturbing possibility that this had been "a crude ploy at effectively trumping a pesky competitor out of the race and thus eliminating a potential funding threat?"[14]

At this point, Pert resigned from NIMH to develop Peptide T on her own but as she freely admits, she did not have one iota of business or political sense. She fought with the NIMH for the license to develop her Peptide T and eventually, in a punishing move, "they also gave joint licensing rights — unprecedented then and now for any drug — to a tiny Canadian company that had none of the qualifications we had. What the government had done, in effect, was to insure that we would not be able to get any mainstream funding for further development, as no other drug company with the millions to invest would ever support research it could not own in its entirety, for obvious reasons."[15]

Pert did however succeed in making a deal with "The Second Biggest Drug Company on the Planet" and they conducted small phase I trials with Peptide T, which were promising but before sizable phase II trials were ever done, the big company pulled out of the deal to pursue a more conventional toxic bomb type of AIDS drug. Now at the end of the road, Pert was faced with the hard realization that her earlier political naïveté and the resulting backlash had shut her out of any support from her former peers.

THE BODYMIND

What may end up being recognized as the most important aspect of Pert's work is her scientific mapping and understanding of what she calls the bodymind. Pert's revolutionary view is that the three classically separated areas of neuroscience, endocrinology, and immunology, with their various organs, the brain; the glands; and the spleen, bone marrow, and lymph nodes are joined to each other in a multidirectional network of communication, linked by information carriers called neuropeptides. She speculates that mind is the flow of information, via neuropeptides among the cells, organs and systems of the body, that body and mind are inseparable and would be more aptly called the bodymind, a term she borrows from alternative health practitioner/acupuncturist, Dianne Connelly:

> In the early days of our professional relationship, [husband] Michael had asked me what I meant by the term neuropeptide. Why add the prefix neuro,

he argued, if the same peptide is found in the gut and immune system, as well as the brain? And why call it a neuroreceptor if it is also found in the gut, in the immune system, alongside the spinal cord, and who knows where else? By tossing out these linguistic distinctions and simply using the term peptides or *information substances* to refer to all peptides regardless of where they occurred, it became more obvious that we were describing a bodywide communication system, one we suspected was ancient in origin, representing the organism's first try at sharing information across cellular barriers. The brain, or neuro, was only one part of the organism's nonhierarchical system to gather, process, and share information (although by far the most complicated and sophisticated component by far).[16]

It is important to note that immune cells do not merely have receptors for these various *information substances*, they also *make, store, and secrete* the neuropeptides themselves. **Immune cells make the same chemicals that are known to control mood in the brain.** Besides controlling the tissue-integrity of the body, immune cells also manufacture information chemicals that can regulate mood or emotion.

In the 1950s, Norwegian-born founder of Biodynamic Psychology and Psychotherapy, Gerda Boyesan created an entire discipline of physical and psychological therapy, based on the idea that the human unconscious resides in the intestines, an idea that is supported by Pert's research. The intestines happen to be an area extremely rich in neuropeptide receptors.

ARE WE ADDICTED TO OUR EMOTIONS?

Nowhere in her book does Pert claim that emotions are addictive. However, this is a very interesting idea that is common in the language of the recovery movement, relating to people's emotional addictions to substances, such as marijuana, or behaviors, such as rage, that are not technically addictive in and of themselves, the way nicotine or heroin physically are. What this generally refers to is a vicious cycle of stimulating one's adrenal glands by any number of means, such as caffeine, sugar or cocaine, anger, fear, vigorous exercise or drama, whether in real-life or via entertainment. Cortisol secreted by the adrenals produces euphoria. It is said that understanding how substances, habits and even emotions affect the adrenal glands can be a key to understanding their addictive power. Over-stimulation eventually weakens the adrenals, causing a deepening of the addiction. Fatigue and depression are often associated with exhausted adrenal glands.

There are also substances and activities that can stimulate the body's release of its own opiate, endorphins, such as chocolate, chili peppers, exercise and sex, all of which are potentially addictive for this reason.

My guess is that the "We are addicted to our emotions" motif is taught at the Ramtha School of Enlightenment. Joe Dispenza, D.C. (Doctor of Chiropractic) expounds on this topic at length in *What The Bleep Do We Know!?* in combination with some of Candace Pert's additional findings, which we will take a brief look at in the following chapter.

CHAPTER 13
JOSEPH DISPENZA, D.C. &
NEUROPEPTIDE ADDICTION

*"I don't think that unless I was creating my day
to have unlimited thought, that that thought
would come."*

Joe Dispenza, D.C.
(Doctor of Chiropractic Medicine), Life University

INVISIBLE SHIPS

At the time of this writing, Dispenza has not yet published his first book but it appears that he lectures regularly at the Ramtha School of Enlightenment on brain science. Many of Dispenza's interview excerpts in the film are extrapolations on the work of Candace Pert, including the unfortunate reference to the native Arawaks' inability to see Columbus' ships when he "discovered" America, in the Bahamas. This old saw circulated around New Age expos in the early 1990s and I was surprised to see two references to it in the film. It is a hackneyed, New Age urban legend, whose source no one has yet been able to trace. There is no historical basis for this story in the records that remain of Columbus' first voyage, all of which are derived from a third-hand transcription of Columbus' written account.

SO, ARE WE ADDICTED TO OUR EMOTIONS OR WHAT?

Happily, Dispenza traffics largely in more edifying ideas, such as the idea that "we are addicted to our emotions,"

177

which appears to be his baby:

> …my definition of an addiction is something really simple; it's something that you can't stop… [which] means that if you can't control your emotional state, you must be addicted to it…

> Emotions are not bad. They are life. They color the richness of our experience. It's our addiction that's the problem…the thing that most people don't realize is that when they understand that they are addicted to emotions, it's not just psychological, it's biochemical. Think about this: heroin uses the same reception mechanisms on the cells as our emotional chemicals use. It's easy to see then, if we can be addicted to heroin, then we can be addicted to any neural peptide, any emotion.[1]

Is this a scientifically proven statement? No. Is it an interesting idea worthy of consideration and perhaps even working on within ourselves? I think so, yes.

NEURAL NETS

Another component of chemical addiction that is illustrated so well by Dispenza's description, in conjunction with digital animation, is the formation of neural nets in the brain around certain thoughts. This appears to be Dispenza's baby, as well, since the term "neural net" usually refers to computers and not to organic brain structures:

> The brain is made up of tiny nerve cells called neurons. These neurons have tiny branches that reach out and connect with other neurons

to form a neural net. Each place where they connect is integrated into a thought or a memory...We know physiologically that nerve cells that fire together wire together. If you practice something over and over again, those nerves have a long-term relationship. If you get angry on a daily basis, if you are frustrated on a daily basis, if you suffer on a daily basis, if you give reason for the victimization in your life, you're re-wiring and re-integrating that neural net on a daily basis and that neural net now has a long term relationship with all those other nerve cells, called an identity. We also know that nerve cells that don't fire together, no longer wire together, they lose their long-term relationship.[2]

Dispenza's ideas here also are very compelling and worthy of consideration, even if they may not be medically proven.

DR. JOE CREATES HIS DAY

Joe Dispenza gets more screen time than any other person in *What The Bleep Do We Know!?* Although there may be scientists who are more illustrious in the film, this chiropractor, who received his degree from a place called Life University, shows himself to be a highly effective communicator. His Joe Six-Pack accessibility demonstrates that if a regular guy can understand all this neuroscience stuff, then so can you! At the *What The Bleep* conference in Boulder, his Regular Joe appeal, coupled with a cute sense of humor, made him one of the more engaging speakers at the event.

It will be interesting to see if the success of *What The*

Bleep Do We Know!? catapaults Dispenza into the New Age stratosphere and helps breathe new life into a movement many thought was over. Dispenza may yet become the Marianne Williamson or Deepak Chopra of the new millennium.

CHAPTER 14
RAMTHA vs. RELIGION

"Do I think you're bad? I don't think you're bad. Do I think you're good? I don't think you're good, either. I think you're God."

Ramtha
Master Teacher — Ramtha School of Enlightenment
Channeled by JZ Knight

IS *WHAT THE BLEEP* A RECRUITMENT FILM FOR RAMTHA?

The most common criticism of **What The Bleep Do We Know!?** is that it is "an infomercial for a controversial New Age sect."[1] Producer-director Will Arntz has constantly found himself having to dispel the rumor that JZ Knight, his astronomically wealthy guru, financed the film. Over and over again, he has explained that he was obliged to reach into his own pocket for the $5 million to produce the movie when he was unable to sell his script to any distributors.

> **Arntz:** Ramtha and the folks at the school had nothing to do with the conception, writing or production of this movie. So to say that this is some sort of Ramtha recruitment film is simply not true. Now I can understand why some people are touchy about that...**It makes sense to me that people would be bothered by something that they felt was trying to get them into some weird cult. I would be bothered by that.** But we were really careful when we were

making this film to stress the idea that it was about the message, not the messenger. Ramtha was not the focal point, just one of the people we interviewed.[2]

Arntz and his collaborators, who are all students at the Ramtha School of Enlightenment (RSE), must feel that they have obtained much of value from their studies with Ramtha. They must have known that there would be Hell to pay for splicing the entity amid highbrow university professors. It was a pretty ballsy move.

Pavel Mikoloski, former RSE Communications Director and now Marketing Director for the film's production house, Captured Light Industries, jokes that if it was supposed to be a recruitment film for Ramtha, "then we did a horrible job!"

The very idea of Ramtha is a tough sell for most people. Even those who are OK with the concept of channeling might not come away with a positive impression of Ramtha after viewing the film, for no other reason than his spurious British accent.

I was more favorably impressed by the talk I saw JZ Knight give (as herself) at the *What the Bleep* conference in April, 2005 in Boulder, Colorado. What a pro! I am somewhat resistant to the Ramtha motif but have determined that, never having been myself to the ranch in Yelm, I am not qualified to judge the RSE. They do a bang-up business over there, thousands of satisfied customers. The DVD that was provided to every attendee of Knight's talk, shows some of what goes on at the ranch and it appears that Ramtha's fundamental tenet is to love and to trust oneself and to get on with the business of having a great life. If the methods and aesthetics espoused at the RSE work for some people, let them have at it, I say.

Clearly, Arntz and his collaborators and the many physicists and other scientists who routinely speak at RSE are not stupid. In fact, most of the scientists interviewed in the film have spoken at the school. Their books and what these scientists teach is part of the curriculum at the Ramtha School of Enlightenment.

> It has taken a long time for my family, myself, and these people to hold their dignity in the face of such outrageous opposition. And we are proud today to come together to celebrate with you an option to meet an outrageous entity that, if you like what he says, will teach you how to become the master of your own destiny. Whether you learn it or not is up to you. Whether you accept it or not is up to you; nobody has to.[3]

After studying RSE, the University of Virginia's Religious Movements Homepage concluded:

> Although Ramtha's School of Enlightenment is surrounded by controversy, there is no clear evidence that JZ is a fraud or that the school is a danger to anyone. Sociologists and psychologists do not believe that students are "brainwashed" to follow this movement, nor are they held against their will. Ramtha's students are searching for answers to life's most important questions, and the School is helping them resolve these issues. Until undisputable evidence arises that JZ is harming people, the media and anti-cultists should be careful with their criticisms.[4]

ATLANTIS AND ALTERNATIVE HISTORY

The controversial figure of Ramtha is the entity who is "channeled" by New Age entrepreneur-powerhouse JZ Knight, who speaks with varying degrees of a quasi-Anglo-Indian accent throughout the film. The entity describes himself as the "the great Ram of the Hindu people,"[5] who incarnated only once as a human being and taught himself how to *ascend*, i.e., to raise his "bodily vibrations into light...[taking his] entire embodiment with [him],"[6] thereby escaping the all-too human experience of death. This purportedly occurred about 35,000 years ago in Earth history, during the era directly preceding the destruction of Atlantis. This flies in the face of the accepted archeological and paleontological chronologies, which tell us that this was the timeframe when Cro-Magnons were painting cute animals in Spanish caves, as well as the Hindu cosmology, which dates the life of the avatar Rama at roughly 5,000 years ago. Atlantis is considered to be a place of Greek legend by most Western historians, not an actual place. Lemuria is not even addressed by mainstream historians.

There is no shortage of alternative historians who claim that our chronologies are incorrect, that carbon dating produces questionable data and that the ancient religious texts used a symbolic language to describe periods of time. For example, the "six days" of Genesis, when God created the heavens and the Earth, are interpreted by some to correspond to the six geological eras in Earth science.

In Western history, the most well-known references to Atlantis come from the ancient Greek accounts of Plato (427–347 BCE), whose works *Critias* and *Timaeus* refer to a sunken continent in the Atlantic Ocean (from which its name derives), which had been destroyed by a natural disaster about 9,000 years before his own time. 19th Century Russian mystic Helena Blavatsky described the civilizations of Atlantis and Lemuria in great detail in her books *Isis Unveiled* and *The Secret Doctrine.* Her information was allegedly based on accounts from ancient Tibetan manuscripts. In the 1930s, Edgar Cayce, the "Sleeping Prophet," spontaneously began trance channeling and gave many accounts of Atlantis, of which he would have no recall when he was out of his trance state.

The word "Lemuria" was coined in the mid-19th Century by the English geologist Philip Sclater when he wrote an article in *The Quarterly Journal of Science,* entitled "The Mammals of Madagascar," explaining why the rare, primordial primate class of lemurs were only found in Madagascar and India, but not in Africa or the Middle East. He theorized that Madagascar and India were once part of a larger, now sunken continent, which he named "Lemuria," after the animals found only there. In the 1930s, British Colonel James Churchward wrote of the ancient civilization of "Mu," which he said was the name of the land which is now located beneath the Pacific. His information was allegedly based on ancient Indian writings.

The Tamil cultures of Southern India today link their ancient traditions of *Kumari Kandam* with Sclater's lost continent of Lemuria, which he theorized was located in the area of the Indian Ocean and South Pacific. The epics *Shilappadikaram* and *Manimekhalai* describe the submerged city of *Puhar* and tell how the Tamil peoples originally came from a submerged island, *Kumarikhandam* off the southern coast of India. Interestingly enough, submerged ruins have recently been found in the ocean near Chennai.

Worldwide, there are hundreds of traditions in many cultures about catastrophes that destroyed the civilization preceding that of the present era. Noah's flood is one of them. Blavatsky claimed that the real chronologies of these stories were suppressed because they discredited the Creationism of the Bible, which claims that the Earth and all life on it were formed in less than a week, 6,000 years ago. She said that both Lemuria and Atlantis were worldwide civilizations and that these terms relate not so much to "places" as to timeframes going back millions of years, when the continental arrangement on the Earth's surface was different. None of this has been proven by geology or archeology and it is unclear why these stories would continue to be "suppressed" in the 21st Century, if they were true. It is worthwhile to note that successive archeological and paleontological discoveries keep pushing human chronology further back in time.

The intention here is not to be an apologist for any faith, whether historical, scientific, religious or spiritualist. As ludicrous as Ramtha, Atlantis or "channeling" may sound to some people, these things are hardly limited to the "New Age." JZ Knight's experiences with Ramtha are similar to those of the prophet Mohammed, whose channeled messages from the Archangel Gabriel produced the Holy Koran of the world's estimated 2 billion Muslims. The 12-million-member-strong LDS Church of Mormonism was similarly founded on the channeled teachings of the angel Moroni to founder Joseph Smith. The Book of Daniel in the Old Testament of Judaism and Christianity describes his encounter with an angel, which is similar to JZ Knight's first encounter with Ramtha. Interestingly, the Bible's account of the after-effects of Daniel's meeting with the shining entity leaves Daniel in a similarly exhausted state to that of Knight after a channeling session:

> His body also was like the beryl, and his face as the appearance of lightning, and his eyes as lamps of fire, and his arms and his feet like in colour to polished brass, and the voice of his words like the voice of a multitude.

> And I Daniel alone saw the vision: for the men that were with me saw not the vision; but a great quaking fell upon them, so that they fled to hide themselves.

> Therefore I was left alone, and saw this great vision, and there remained no strength in me: for my comeliness was turned in me into corruption, and I retained no strength.

> Yet heard I the voice of his words: and when I heard the voice of his words, then was I in a deep sleep on my face, and my face toward the ground.[7]

In a report comparing JZ Knight to other women spiritual leaders over the past 150 years, such as Mary Baker Eddy, founder of the Church of Christian Science, and Helena Blavatsky, creator of the Theosophical Society, and the obstacles they faced in spreading their systems of teachings, Gail Harley, Ph.D., a professor of religious studies from the University of South Florida, says "... don't forget that all religions were new at one time."

FRAUD INVESTIGATION ACQUITS JZ KNIGHT

Psychologists, sociologists and religious experts from Temple University, Colgate University, the University of

California, the University of Oregon, Chicago Theological Seminary and Birbeck College at the University of London studied JZ Knight before, during, and after channeling Ramtha. During a year-long period between 1996 and 1997, Knight risked her reputation by subjecting herself to a battery of physiological and psychological tests. It was determined that she was not faking the effects of the spiritual possession of her body and that it would have been impossible for her to have simultaneously faked all of the many alterations of her various vital signs.

> This doesn't prove Ramtha, but what it does say is that there is a phenomenon that is occurring here that cannot be play-acted and cannot be written off as another aspect of my personality.[8]

RAMTHA AND THE INSTITUTE OF NOETIC SCIENCES

Ramtha's basic teachings are consistent with those of the Human Potential Movement, which developed out of the Humanistic Psychology of Abraham Maslow during Knight's youth in the social tumult of the 1960s at places such as the Esalen Institute and the Institute of Noetic Sciences, both in Northern California. The Human Potential Movement is based on the idea that human beings have vast untapped potentials for extraordinary abilities, which can be developed by ridding themselves of limiting beliefs. By cultivating their potential it is thought that individuals can transform the world into a better place.

The Institute of Noetic Sciences (IONS) was involved in putting together the Study Guide[9] for **What The Bleep Do We Know!?** and is a sponsor of the Prophet's Conference lecture tour featuring the scientists from the film. Many of the scientists interviewed have been previously affiliated with the IONS in some way. William Tiller, Ph.D. is a founding director; Amit Goswami is a Senior Scholar in Residence; Fred Alan Wolf, John Hagelin and Candace Pert speak there regularly; along with other fixtures in the New Age lecture circuit who do not appear in the film, like Deepak Chopra and Marianne Williamson.

The Institute of Noetic Sciences was founded in 1973 by NASA Apollo 14 astronaut, Edgar Mitchell, Ph.D. to sponsor research into the nature of consciousness, after his own life-changing experiences on the Moon and in Outer Space, where among other things, he witnessed UFOs. Mitchell was vocal about these experiences and the way this phenomenon was being handled by the authorities:

> ...he is 90 per cent sure that many of the thousands of unidentified flying objects, or UFOs, recorded since the 1940s, belong to visitors "from other planets" and that UFO's have been the "subject of disinformation in order to deflect attention and to create confusion so the truth doesn't come out."[10]

The Human Potential Movement does have its critics. In his incisive essay, psychotherapist Geoffrey Hill, who has lectured several times at Esalen says that for all of its noble and revolutionary intentions, the Human Potential Movement appears to have now stagnated. He criticizes the movement for promoting infantilism, narcissism, feel-good experientialism, denial, anti-intellectualism and being lightweight and overly optimistic. He observes that the Boomer generation that was the exponent of the HPM has since settled into conformist lifestyles, based on surviving economically and emotionally in an unstable world. "By the time most persons have reached middle age, they have been so battered and bruised by life's incessant blows, they try not to rock the boat, lest the little comfort they have attained be taken away from them."

...the [Human Potential Movement] was born at the coming of age of the baby boom generation, a transcendentally hungry generation, ready for new ideas. The first wave of baby boomers to come of age in the 1960s was like a tribe of spiritual pioneers, searching for new vistas of human experience. Thousands were caught up in cults, new religions and political movements. The first generation born after the shock of World War II was ready and willing to try new ways of being, whether through spirituality, drugs, sex or activism. It was the generation which, unlike all before it, demanded honesty, integrity and authentic reality, even if they had to transcend reality to make it more real.

...the sad reality is, only a very small minority of the boom generation have actually realized authentic human potentiality. The majority of the generation, even those who experimented heavily with alternative realities, have seriously compromised their quest and have settled for rather mediocre lifestyles of bourgeois comfort. If potentiality has been attained, it has been found far more in personal career and financial rewards than in the invisible, altruistic, or higher-state side of the equation of which Abraham Maslow spoke.

One of the grand successes of the Human Potential Movement has been that it has attracted a very loyal following of dedicated boomers forever attached to feel-good experiences. There is no doubt that the movement has been immensely successful in perpetuating a mass addiction to experiences of feeling good...

I'm convinced that when an atmosphere is created which puts an extreme emphasis on experience over understanding, that atmosphere will inevitably create and encourage infantile selfishness.[11]

YOU ARE GOD

What distinguishes Ramtha's teachings from some other great American self-help modalities of the late 20th Century, such as Alcoholics Anonymous and its numerous offshoots; Scientology; est/Landmark Education; etc., is RSE's specific emphasis on the idea that "You are God." Although the real meaning of this statement is probably more like "God is within you," the insistence on the phrase "You are God" could have an almost hypnotic effect, tricking the ego and the subconscious into thinking that they are actually God, which would doubtless have some impact on one's conduct. It could be argued that if God is All That Is, then we all ARE God, the same way that a speck of dust is God.

The Buddhist greeting of putting hands in prayer, signals the recognition of the Divine within the person being greeted. Perhaps if we all saw the God in each other, the world would be a better place. If we saw a messed-up person and saw that as God having a hard time expressing through that person, it might transform the way we relate to one another...

Another distinguishing feature of RSE's methods is the use of quantum physics terminology to support the "You are God" and such correlates as "you create your own reality." The "observer effect" in quantum physics experiments is invoked to support the idea that it is the God aspect within the observer who causes subatomic wavefunction collapse, which thereby "creates reality." This is more or less the hypothesis of Amit Goswami's "monistic idealism," detailed in a separate chapter of this book.

Pop star quantum physicist Fred Alan Wolf, Ph.D. is evidently a fan of Ramtha's, as evidenced by the introduction he gives on the Ramtha – Create Your Day: An Invitation to Open Your Mind DVD, directed by What the Bleep Co-Director Mark Vicente and released in March 2005:

> How a 35,000-year-old wisdom warrior has come to be so well-versed in quantum physics is a delight. In today's world where presidents lie and intelligence networks distort truth, it is refreshing to realize that a deeper reality exists and that someone we can actually believe has access to it. Listen and watch Ramtha. You will get closer to the truth than you can from many of today's resources. **Oh, by the way, you will also learn how you create your reality.**[12]

"Manifesting" wealth and health are seen as signs that the student is successfully tapping inner divinity. If one contracts cancer or a common cold, one is seen to be "vibrating at the same frequency" as the disease. Failure to prevent the aging process or that of disease is a failure to master Ramtha's teachings. (From the little that I have witnessed of Knight and her students, it does not appear that anyone at RSE has thoroughly mastered these teachings yet). The ultimate test of self-mastery would be ascension:

> Those who have ascended this plane have mastered the ultimate, which is death. They have learned how to raise, through the power of their thought the vibratory frequency of the body's molecular structures to the point where the body is taken with them into a light existence, thus forever bypassing death...when you take the body with you, the body can be raised and lowered upon any frequency level you choose. So if you choose to come back into this frequency, you never have to look for another body, with another ego, in order to exist in another life, with another family, in another country. You no longer have to be born again into this plane of limited thinking only to undergo the programming of social consciousness and have to fight for the expression of self in order to regain your knowingness. You do not have to learn all over again that the body can be restored to the purest light-form from which it came. You do not have to learn again that this is just an illusion and a game.
>
> Once you master ascension, you maintain your body forever and can come and go at will with your own embodiment. Then any moment you wish to be part of this plane again, all you have to do is lower the bodily vibrations to where it vibrates at the same frequency as this plane, and here you are.

All here are capable of ascending, for that which lurks behind the illusion of flesh is the creator of all the universes. And you at your choosing can make this manifestation occur... ascension is very easy to achieve. In truth, it is simpler than dying. What is difficult to achieve is mastering judgment against your thoughts. What is difficult to achieve is mastering the illusion of time in order to allot yourself the patience to do it. But once you do, ascension is simply a thought away. Then you have retained your body for all times and can thus be a traveler upon any plane at any moment you choose.[13]

RAMTHA VS. RELIGION VS. RAMTHA

Another controversial aspect of **What The Bleep Do We Know!?** which is consistent with Ramtha's teachings is the rather surly treatment of religion in the film, which producer-director Will Arntz describes as trying to "kick religion in the nuts":

Interviewer: Did you go to church as a child?

Arntz: Yes I did and it was responsible for me turning off to most spiritual stuff... Which is why we have that section in the film where we try to "kick religion in the nuts" as I like to say. I just think that there are a lot of people in this country who are very spiritual but were just turned off to religion at a young age. Because they could think. So they just walked away from the whole thing. But now many are coming back. On their own terms. Willing to distill the difference between religion and spirituality. Religion says, "My way or the Hell way." We are saying, "There are six billion people on the planet. Six billion ways."[14]

From a fundamentalist Christian website, we find a very clear, if opinionated description of the 180-degree difference between the Christian path and the mystical approach promoted in the film and by Ramtha:

> For the Christian, salvation is based on something entirely outside of man. Salvation is found in the faithfulness and perfect sacrifice of the Christ of history…**Eastern mystics claim to discover God in the depths of their being. The true Christian looks away from himself to the righteousness of Christ Jesus.**
>
> The deadly deceptions of mysticism arrogantly advertise a way of direct access to the All Holy God and thereby repudiate any need of the Lord Jesus Christ, the One Mediator between God and men…
>
> True faith involves a repudiation of the self-deceit of experiential mystical means of reaching God, "for there is one God, and one mediator between God and men, the man Christ Jesus." The Lord Jesus stands ready to receive every sinner who will throw away his rebellion and pride and trust in Him alone for salvation![15]

Ramtha would be in complete agreement with the above statement — except to say that it was Christianity that was "deadly deceptive," by advertising that access to God could be achieved only by belief in Jesus Christ, "the One Mediator between God and men."

Miceal Ledwith, a learned man who now lectures at RSE, was previously a Monsignor of the Catholic Church, an advisor to the Holy See, a Professor of Systematic Theology and President of Maynooth College in Ireland for over 20 years, appears in the film and also lectures at the *What The Bleep* conferences. The gist of his talks is one of grave wounding at the hands of the Church, which appears to be similar to the experience of JZ Knight, Arntz and of many people seeking answers at places like RSE. However, those who have not suffered as a result of religion may be taken aback by the church bashing that goes on in **What The Bleep Do We Know!?**

BEYOND GOOD AND EVIL

At various times during the film, Ramtha and Ledwith express another fundamental precept of the Ramtha School of Enlightenment: "there really is no such thing as good or bad." Many people have a problem with this idea because it can only make sense outside of the context of one's moral values, from a state of complete detachment from a human agenda and human judgment.

> ...the mystical journey consists in transcending all dualities, including the one of evil and good... Mysticism...does not dichotomize between and heaven and hell; both are natural concomitants of how we live.[16]

Transcending duality is not to be confused with condoning the violation of anybody's rights, such as Charles Manson did when he justified his acts of murder by saying, "If God is One, what is bad?" Transcending duality is an inner, contemplative activity, which can help people to "think outside of the box" to solve their problems. The insights obtained from this mystical state of mind are unrelated to the necessary behavioral and legal codes that make up the fabric of society.

At least, this is how I understand it. Hopefully, Ledwith agrees with me, and I also hope that the statement, "there really is no such thing as good or bad" is not simply his way of justifying the alleged sexual molestation that he was accused of on more than one occasion,[17] around the time he left the Church, left Ireland and dropped the "h" from his first name.

I would probably hate the Church, too, if it meant my being in an environment where I would be constantly subjected to unfounded sexual abuse allegations…

> The typical New Age notion is that you want good things to happen to you, so think good thoughts; and because your create your own reality, those thoughts will come true. Conversely, if you are sick, it's because you have been bad. **The mystical notion, on the other hand, is that your deepest Self transcends both good and bad, so by accepting absolutely everything that happens to you – by equally embracing both good and bad with equanimity – you can transcend the ego altogether.** The idea is…to gently rise above both [good and bad].[18]

COPYRIGHTED SPIRIT

Speaking of the law, JZ Knight has proven to be very good at wielding it. In 1997, she won a ruling from the Austrian Supreme Court against a woman who claimed to channel Ramtha in German in a precedent-setting copyright and trademark infringement case.

"Trademarks are designed to protect the public from false and misleading claims," says Ms. Knight when asked why she pressed the case to the Supreme Court of a foreign country. "I didn't want the German-speaking people of Europe to be misled by someone who, under the name of Ramtha, was distorting his teachings and in some cases teaching things that were directly opposite of his teachings. It is up to me to keep the teachings pure and uncorrupted and I take my job quite seriously, as you can see. I am overjoyed that the Supreme Court upheld the decision."[19]

HOW MUCH IS RAMTHA WORTH?

Few stories focus on the amazing success of the JZ Knight phenomenon. Judith Darlene Hampton, the rags-to-riches entrepreneurial dynamo, was born the eighth child of nine to impoverished parents who picked cotton and lived in a one-room shack in New Mexico. The "Z" comes from "Zebra," a nickname she received for her ability to make "black and white" decisions. Though her companies will not publicly disclose their operations' income, "one observer pegs its annual income at $10 million at least."[20] Of that amount, $4.5 million would be exclusively from the $1,500 yearly fees paid by her 3,000 established students for their required yearly group retreat and follow-up, per the information posted on the Ramtha site.[21]

Besides the numerous Ramtha books, videos and audio recordings, a dizzying array of items can be purchased from the four JZK-affiliated websites, from "Elfin" magical capes and wizard robes ("Elegant cloaks that Radiate Nobility")[22] to furniture and bath products sold from seventeen separate shops in a virtual 19th Century village.[23] The overall vibe of the JZK websites and their products is romantic and fantastical.

As Knight has been at it since the late-1970s, that would make her a kind of Bill Gates — or at least an Oprah Winfrey — of the New Age business. It would certainly indicate that she has mastered the "manifestation" of wealth. But she is probably also the hardest-working woman in the New Age business, allowing herself to be possessed by an entity half the time and having thousands of students trampling through her ranch every year...

People are skeeved by the association of business with spirituality, holding onto an idea that spiritual leaders should be ascetic penitents who take vows of poverty. This is seldom the case. As evidenced with billionaire *Washington Times* owner, Sun Myung Moon and his Unification Church, Jim and Tammy Faye Bakker and their PTL, Maharishi Mahesh Yogi's several organizations and countless other examples, the spiritual institution is a great business model! Rarely is it pointed out that the Catholic Church may be the world's single wealthiest establishment.

There is no question that, as successful as Knight has already been, the film has exposed a larger audience to Ramtha than ever before — though the same could certainly be said of the physicists and most of the actors in the film, as well.

CONCLUSION

IS GOD AN OUTLAW?

Perhaps the fundamental debate stirred up by **What The Bleep Do We Know!?** is the question of whether or not free will exists. Orthodox science would suggest that there is no such thing. In David Albert's view, for example, to equate quantum physics with "free will" is childish, wishful thinking. He was "bothered" and "saddened" that the filmmakers who promoted this idea were "exploiting" the demand for a "reassuring and accessible image of ourselves,"[1] as he said during his talk in Santa Monica.

While the determinist worldview may seem bleak to some, others find solace in the idea that there is no free will. Lack of freedom signifies that personal responsibility is an illusion, which is paradoxically freeing. The mechanistic universe is a cozy, closed system, made up of predictable laws, where one can only do what one can do. All doubts about what one could have done are moot. Total certainty can be very comforting, especially because it is bolstered by so much scientific evidence.

> The idea that the entire universe is nothing more than a "physical system" — that is, a machine — unfolding mechanically according to rigid and immutable laws began as the radical heresy of a few brave minds. With this idea as their starting point, they and their followers began to experience an uninterrupted string of successes. **There is not a single working medical device or treatment, not a vehicle, not a communications technology, not an industry that isn't based on this assumption.**[2]

But the indeterminacy in quantum mechanics appeals to those wishing to rescue a sense of free will from a mechanistic universe:

> The resemblance between quantum mechanics and certain aspects of Eastern philosophy was recognized by some of the architects of the theory themselves. But these speculations remained outside the mainstream until physicist and systems theorist Fritjof Capra's 1975 book *The Tao of Physics* heralded a contemporary movement that sought to fuse quantum physics and spirituality.[3]

As Jeffrey Satinover says, the belief or non-belief in free will may be a matter of taste, style or "preference":

> Either it is absolute chance or absolute will...Both are equally mysterious as explanations go. Indeed, they are hardly even that: **They are merely terms for something beyond our ken. You might as well call it the Tao — or Ralph.**[4]

But if a "spiritualist" vision of the world is true; that thoughts do "matter," that souls are "real" and there is a "God," then energetic principles and laws that describe these phenomena may one day be defined, as some of the scientists interviewed in the film are attempting to do. Perhaps a Theory of Everything, a mathematical description for All That Is will one day be definitively proved. But what if infinity is not a closed system of laws? Would the idea of "freedom" imply that "God" is an outlaw?

SPIRITUAL CINEMA

The more I think about the ideas discussed and the choices

that they made to express them, the more I admire **What The Bleep Do We Know!?** and its filmmakers.

That Arntz, Chasse and Vicente have motivated people to read these books and to ponder these ideas is more than commendable. Numerous study groups are said to have formed from Jacksonville, Florida to Queensland, Australia.

That a theatrical audience was for once not treated like a bunch of bloodthirsty ignoramuses or maudlin saps is conclusively a positive development and I sincerely hope their vision of a "spiritual cinema" takes off. It will be most interesting to see what these filmmakers do next.

> Cinema — the art form of the Modern World — has only brushed the surface of the depth of information, material and revelations that lurk within the marvelous spiritual traditions and mysteries around the world. We think it's time for a change.[5]

FURTHER READING/ VIEWING

THE OFFICIAL BOOKS

There are two "official" books from the makers of **What The Bleep Do We Know!?**:

• *The Little Book of Bleeps* by William Arntz and Betsy Chasse (Editors), published by Captured Light Distribution/ Beyond Words Publishing (2004)

• *What The Bleep Do We Know: Discovering The Endless Possibilities for Altering Your Everyday Reality* by William Arntz, Betsy Chasse and Mark Vicente with Jack Forem (Nov. 2005), published by Health Communications, Inc.

The first book, *The Little Book of Bleeps*, is really just a picture book with some small quotes, so it is a good gift item but won't satisfy anyone looking for more information on the themes in the film.

Although not published at the time of this writing, based on an early sample provided to me by the publisher, the second book will be much more comprehensive and probably a "must-have" for those seriously interested in applying the themes in the movie to real life. A large, hardcover book in full color, it will contain quotes, illustrations, movie stills, interviews and exercises.

THE MOVIE AND DVD

Another development to look forward to is the theatrical release of a three-hour extended version of the movie, scheduled for January-February 2006 in the United States, followed in March 2006 by a deluxe DVD release of the extended movie plus extras, from Fox Home Video.

THE WEB SITE

The filmmakers have created an elaborate and very interesting website and I encourage all readers to surf around the site and click on all the links. There is too much on the site to mention everything here, but among other items are the Study Guide, discussed below, information about all the conferences and even what they describe as the "first organic virtual reality movie plaza in entertainment history." See: http://www.whatthebleep.com.

STUDY GUIDE

The makers of **What The Bleep Do We Know!?**, in conjunction with The Institute of Noetic Sciences (IONS), have created a Study Guide, which can be downloaded from this webpage: http://www.whatthebleep.com/guide/

The Study Guide is quite extensive and those seeking more information will certainly want to download and read the entire guide. However, below I have included some of the recommended further reading from the Guide, much of which also formed my reference material in writing this book.

What The Bleep Do We Know!? — Study Guide Recommended Reading: For Holding Group Dialogues

BOOKS

Bohm, David. 1999. *On Dialogue*. (Routledge)

Ellinor, Linda, and Gerard, Glenna. 1998. *Dialogue: Rediscover the Transforming Power of Conversation*. (John Wiley and Sons, Inc.)

Hammond, Sue Annis. 1998. *Thin Book of Appreciative Inquiry*. (Thin Book)

Isaacs, William. 1999. *Dialogue: The Art of Thinking Together*. (Doubleday)

Jaida N'Ha, Sandra. 1997. *The Joy of Conversation*. (Utne)

The *Utne Reader*–sponsored guide to co-creative salons of all types. Excellent write-ups on study circles, listening circles, and more. See also: www.utne.com

Oliver, Leonard P. 1987. *Study Circles: Coming Together for Personal Growth and Social Change*. (Seven Locks Press)

INTERNET
For an informative list distinguishing dialogue from debate, see Dialogue vs. Debate on the Canada's National Adult Literacy Database: www.nald.ca/clr/study/scdvd.htm

For a general description of many types of dialogue and facilitation, see the dialogue and facilitation pages of the Co-Intelligence Institute's website. www.co-intelligence.org

RESOURCE CENTER
The Study Circle Resource Center, PO Box 203, Pomfret, CT, 06258. Phone (860) 9282616, FAX (860) 928-3713, email scrc@neca.com and www.studycircles.org. Provides training materials, study circle packets, and guidance. Helpful staff. You can ask for their study circle guide "Building Strong Neighborhoods" and the larger neighborhood kit, which has a plan for organizing whole cities, as well as the dialogue guide.

What The Bleep Do We Know!? — Study Guide
Recommended Reading: Paradigm Shifts

BOOKS

Berry, Thomas. 1993. *Dream of the Earth*. (HarperCollins)

Brown, Harrison. 1954. *The Challenge of Man's Future*. (MacMillan)

Conant, Jim, and Haugeland, John, eds. 2000. *The Road Since Structure: Philosophical Essays by Thomas Kuhn, 1970–1993*. (The University of Chicago Press)

De Quincey, Christian. 2005. *Radical Knowing: Exploring Consciousness Through Relationship*. (Inner Traditions)

Gebser, Jean. 1993. *The Ever-Present Origin*. (Ohio University Press)

Harman, Willis. 1988. *Global Mind Change*. (Warner Books)

Kuhn, Thomas S. 1996. *The Structure of Scientific Revolutions*. (The University of Chicago Press)

Laszlo, Ervin. 2004. *Science and the Akashic Field*. (Inner Traditions)

Macy, Joanna. 1991. *World as Lover, World as Self*. (Parallax Press)

Polak, Fred. 1961. *The Image of the Future*. (Oceana Publications)

Schlitz, M., Amorok, T., Micozzi, M. 2005. *Consciousness and Healing*. (Elsevier Press)

Sorokin, Pitirim. 1941. *The Crisis of Our Age*. (E. P. Dutton)

Sorokin, Pitirim. 1993. *Social and Cultural Dynamics*. (Bedminster Press)

Swimme, Brian. 1999. *The Hidden Heart of the Cosmos: Humanity and the New Story.* (Orbis)

Tarnas, Richard. 1991. *The Passion of the Western Mind.* (Harmony Books)

Woodhouse, Mark. 1996. *Paradigm Wars: Worldviews for a New Age.* (Frog Ltd.)

What The Bleep Do We Know!? — Study Guide Recommended Reading: Quantum Mechanics

BOOKS

Davies, P. C. W. 1986. *The Ghost in the Atom: A Discussion of the Mysteries of Quantum Physics.* (Cambridge University Press)

Feynman, Richard. 1985. *QED: The Strange Theory of Light and Matter.* (Princeton University Press)

Greene, Brian. 2000 *The Elegant Universe: Superstrings, Hidden Dimensions, and the Quest for the Ultimate Theory.* (Vintage)

Hawking, Stephen. 1998. *A Brief History of Time: The Updated and Expanded Tenth Anniversary Edition.* (Bantam)

Heisenberg, Werner. 1958. *Physics and Philosophy: The Revolution in Modern Science.* (Harper and Row)

Heisenberg, Werner. 1971. *Physics and Beyond: Encounters and Conversations.* (Harper and Row)

Herbert, Nick. 1987. *Quantum Reality: Beyond the New Physics.* (Anchor Books)

McFarlane, Thomas. Summer-Fall 1999. "The Illusion of Materialism: How Quantum Physics Contradicts the Belief in an Objective World Existing Independent of Observation." *Center Voice: The Newsletter of the Center for Sacred Sciences.*

Zukav, Gary. 1990. *The Dancing Wu Li Masters*. (Bantam Books)

INTERNET

Heisenberg and Uncertainty: A Web Exhibit American Institute of Physics www.aip.org/history/heisenberg/

Measurement in Quantum Mechanics: Frequently Asked Questions edited by Paul Budnik www.mtnmath.com/faq/meas-qm.html

The Particle Adventure: An interactive tour of fundamental particles and forces Lawrence Berkeley National Laboratory www.particleadventure.org

Discussions with Einstein on Epistemological Problems in Atomic Physics, Niels Bohr (1949) www.marxists.org/reference/subject/philosophy/works/dk/bohr.htm

The History of Quantum Theory, Werner Heisenberg (1958) www.marxists.org/reference/subject/philosophy/works/ge/heisenb2.htm

The Copenhagen Interpretation of Quantum Theory, Werner Heisenberg (1958) www.marxists.org/reference/subject/philosophy/works/ge/heisenb3.htm

The Illusion of Materialism by Thomas J. McFarlane www.integralscience.org/materialism/materialism.html

What The Bleep Do We Know!? — **Study Guide Links for General Information on Quantum Mechanics:**

http://en.wikipedia.org/wiki/Quantum_mechanics

http://plato.stanford.edu/entries/qt-quantlog/

http://scienceworld.wolfram.com/physics/topics/
EarlyQuantumMechanics.html

www.benbest.com/science/quantum.html

www.mtnmath.com/faq/meas-qm-0.html

What The Bleep Do We Know!? — **Study Guide**
Recommended Reading: Focusing Intention &
Creating Reality

BOOKS

Allen, Pat. 1999. "Intention and Creativity: Art as Spiritual Practice." In *The Soul of Creativity*, ed. Tona Pearce Myers, 168-176. (New World Library)

Barnhart, Bruno. 1999. *Second Simplicity*, (Paulist Press)

Bolen, Jean Shinoda. 1998. "Synchronistic Knowing: Understanding Meaningful Coincidence." In *Inner Knowing: Consciousness, Creativity, Insight, Intuition*, ed. Helen Palmer, 43-50. (Tarcher/Putnam)

Bohm, David. 2002. *Wholeness and the Implicate Order.* (Routledge; Reissue Edition)

Broughton, Richard S. 1991. *Parapsychology: The Controversial Science*, (Ballantine Books; 1st Edition)

Capra, Fritjof. 2000. *The Tao of Physics.* (Shambhala; 4th Edition)

Csikszentmihalyi, Mihaly. 1988. "Society, Culture and Person: A Systems View of Creativity."— In *The Nature of Creativity*, ed. R. Sternberg, 336. (Cambridge University Press)

Combs, Allan, Holland, Mark. 2000. *Synchronicity: Through the Eyes of Science, Myth and the Trickster.* (Marlowe & Company; 2nd Edition)

Cooper, Rabbi David. 1997. *God is a Verb*. (Penguin Putnam)

Diaz, Adriana. 1999. "Brush with God—Creativity as Practice and Prayer." In *The Soul of Creativity*, ed. Tona Pearce Myers, 177-183. (New World Library)

Goswami, Amit with Richard Reed and Maggie Goswami. 1998. *The Self-Aware Universe: How Consciousness Creates the Material World*. (Tarcher/Putnam)

Jung, Carl. 1973. *Synchronicity*. (Bollingen Paperback Edition)

Nadeau, Robert and Kafatos, Menas. 2001. *The Non-Local Universe: The New Physics and Matters of the Mind*. (Oxford University Press; New Edition)

McTaggart, Lynn. 2003. *The Field: The Quest for the Secret Force of the Universe*. (Perennial Currents).

Montuori, Alfonso and Ronald Purser. 1996. *Social Creativity*, vol. 1 (Hampton Press)

Radin, Dean I. 1997. *The Conscious Universe: The Scientific Truth of Psychic Phenomena*. (HarperSanFrancisco; 1st Edition)

Talbot, Michael. 1992 *The Holographic Universe*. (Perennial; Reprint Edition)

Targ, Russell. 2004. *Limitless Mind: A Guide to Remote Viewing and Transformation of Consciousness*. (New World Library)

Tharp, Twyla. 2003. *The Creative Habit: Learn it and Use it for Life*. (Simon & Schuster)

Ywahoo, Dhyani. 1987. *Voices of Our Ancestors*. (Shambhala; 1st Edition)

Additional Background Information
Recommended by the Author

PHYSICS

BOOKS
Kaku, Michio. 1995. *Hyperspace: A Scientific Odyssey Through Parallel Universes, Time Warps, and the 10th Dimension.* (Anchor)

Penrose, Roger. 2005. *The Road to Reality: A Complete Guide to the Laws of the Universe.* (Knopf)

INTERNET
http://quantumfuture.net/quantum_future/

MYSTICISM, THEOSOPHY & ALCHEMY

Blavatsky, Helena Petrovna. Originally published in 1888. *The Secret Doctrine.* (Quest Books; Reissue Edition)

Cayce, Edgar Evans and Cayce, Hugh Lynn. 1988. *Edgar Cayce on Atlantis.* (Warner Books; Reissue Edition)

Churchward, James. 1988. *The Children of Mu.* (Brotherhood of Life; Reprint Edition)

Fulcanelli. 1999. *The Dwellings of the Philosophers.* (Archive Press & Communications)

Gurdjieff, G.I. 1969. *Meetings With Remarkable Men.* (Arkana S.) (Penguin Books; New Edition)

Kharitidi, Olga. 1997. *Entering the Circle: Ancient Secrets of Siberian Wisdom Discovered by a Russian Psychiatrist.* (HarperSanFrancisco)

Krishnamurti, Jiddu. 1975. *Freedom from the Known.* (HarperSanFrancisco)

Ouspensky, P.D. 2001. *In Search of the Miraculous: Fragments of an Unknown Teaching.* (Harvest/HBJ Book; New Edition)

Velikovsky, Immanuel. 1984. *Worlds in Collision.* (Pocket; Reissue Edition)

CHANNELING

BOOKS

Marciniak, Barbara. 1992. *Bringers of the Dawn: Teachings from the Pleiadians.* (Bear & Company)

Marciniak, Barbara. 1994. *Earth: Pleiadian Keys to the Living Library.* (Bear & Company)

Roberts, Jane. 1994. *The Nature of Personal Reality: Specific, Practical Techniques for Solving Everyday Problems and Enriching the Life You Know.* (Amber-Allen Publishing; Reprint Edition)

Roberts, Jane. 1994. *Seth Speaks: The Eternal Validity of the Soul* (Amber-Allen Publishing; Reprint Edition)

Royal, Lyssa and Priest, Keith. 1993. *The Prism of Lyra: An Exploration of Human Galactic Heritage.* (Light Technology Publications; Revised Edition)

INTERNET
http://www.cassiopaea.com

GLOSSARY

Agonist/Antagonist is a substance that binds to a receptor and triggers a response by the cell. An agonist is the opposite of an antagonist in the sense that while an antagonist also binds to the receptor, it fails to activate the receptor and actually blocks it from activation by agonists.

Assay is a procedure where the concentration of a component part of a mixture is determined.

Atlantis was a legendary ancient culture and island, whose existence and location have never been confirmed. The first mentions we have are from the classical Greek philosopher Plato, who said that it was destroyed by a natural disaster (possibly an earthquake or tsunami) about 9,000 years before his own time. Plato did mention it was somewhere near Hyperborea, which is presumed to be near Iceland, though some think its location would have been more suitable in one of the cradles of civilization, the Mediterranean Sea.

Axon or "nerve fiber," is a long slender projection of a nerve cell, or "neuron," which conducts electrical impulses away from the neuron's cell body or soma. Axons are in effect the primary transmission lines of the nervous system, and as bundles they help make up nerves. Individual axons are microscopic in diameter (typically about one micrometer across) but may extend to macroscopic lengths. The longest axons in the human body, for example, are those of the sciatic nerve, which run from the base of the spine to the big toe of each foot. These single-cell fibers may extend a meter or even longer.

Blavatsky née Helena Petrovna Hahn (1831-1891), better known as Helena Blavatsky or Madame Blavatsky was the founder of Theosophy (See also **Theosophy**).

Bodymind a term first proposed by Dianne Connelly, reflects the understanding, derived from Chinese medicine, that the body is inseparable from the mind.[1]

Bose-Einstein Condensate is a gaseous superfluid phase formed by atoms cooled to temperatures very near to absolute zero, the temperature at which molecular movement stops, which is 0 degrees Kelvin. The first such condensate was produced by Eric Cornell and Carl Wieman in 1995, using a gas of rubidium atoms cooled to 170 nanokelvin (nK). Under such conditions, a large fraction of the atoms collapse into the lowest quantum state, producing a superfluid (which is a phase of matter characterized by the complete absence of viscosity. Thus superfluids, placed in a closed loop, can flow endlessly without friction).

Causal Determinism expresses the belief that every effect has a cause, and therefore science, pursued diligently enough, will explain all natural phenomena and thus produce a TOE (Theory of Everything).

This idea goes hand in hand with materialism. Scientists and skeptics may implicitly favour causal determinism because it does not allow for any supernatural explanations of reality. (See also **Causality**, **Determinism**, **Materialism** and **Theory of Everything**).

Causality is the relationship between causes and effects. Although it is often examined in the fields of philosophy, computer science, and statistics, it has a place in the study of physics as well.

In classical physics, it was assumed that all events are caused by earlier ones according to the known laws of nature, culminating in Pierre-Simon Laplace's claim that if the current state of the world would be known with precision, it could be computed for any time in the future. This is known as determinism.

According to classical physics, the cause simply had to precede its effect. In modern physics, the notion of causality had to be clarified.

The insights of the theory of special relativity confirmed the assumption of causality, but they made the meaning of the word "precede" observer-dependent. Consequently, the relativistic principle of causality says that the cause must precede its effect according to all inertial observers. This is equivalent to the statement that the cause and its effect are separated by a timelike interval, and the effect belongs to the future of its cause. Equivalently, special relativity has shown that it is not only impossible to influence the past; it is also impossible to influence distant objects by signals that are superluminal (faster than light).

In the theory of general relativity, the concept of causality is generalized in the most straightforward way: the effect must belong to the future light cone of its cause, even if the spacetime is curved. New subtleties must be taken into account when we investigate causality in quantum mechanics and relativistic quantum field theory in particular. In quantum field theory, causality is closely related to the principle of locality. A careful analysis of the phenomena is needed, and the outcome slightly depends on the chosen interpretation of quantum mechanics.

Despite these subtleties, causality remains an important and valid concept in physical theories. For example, the notion that events can be ordered into causes and effects is necessary to prevent paradoxes such as the grandfather paradox, which asks what happens if a time-traveller kills his own grandfather before he ever meets his grandmother. (See also **Determinism**).

Channeling According to Webster's Dictionary: the practice of professedly entering a meditative or trancelike state in order to convey messages from a spiritual guide.

In the New Age movement, channeling is the claimed receipt of information or commands by a person functioning as a medium or channel for an unknown or divine source, much as a radio receives a signal from a transmitter. Although the term was coined in the 20th century, the concept is quite old and widespread.

Channeling is often believed to entail spiritual possession, where a spiritual being takes control of the receiving person's body. It may also refer to other psychic phenomena where the patient loses only part of his control on his body, as in certain forms of dowsing, or merely acquires new information or ability, as in clairvoyance and telepathy.

Chiropractic is a health discipline that seeks to prevent and treat health problems by using spinal adjustments in order to correct misalignments, or subluxations. The brain and nervous system control and coordinate all the body's functions in part through nerve branches that exit from the spinal cord between the vertebrae. Slight spinal misalignments are said to interfere with the function of the nerve as it exits the verterbral foramina. Chiropractors were the first to infer a causal relationship between nerve interference or compression at the spine and subsequent problems in more distant parts or organ systems regulated by the nerve.

Practitioners of chiropractic are called *chiropractors*. They receive the degree *Doctor of Chiropractic*, (D.C.) and are commonly called doctor in the same way that a dentist is called a doctor.

This practice has been shown to be effective in treating back and neck pain, headaches, and other symptoms of spine-related conditions.

Some medical doctors and scientists assert that chiropractic treatment is pseudoscience.

Classical Mechanics (or Classical Physics) is one of the two major sub-fields of study in the science of mechanics, which is concerned with the motions of bodies, and the forces that cause them. The other sub-field is quantum mechanics. Roughly speaking, classical mechanics was developed in the 400 years since the groundbreaking works of Brahe, Kepler, and Galilei, while quantum mechanics developed within the last 100 years, starting with similarly decisive discoveries by Planck, Einstein, and Bohr.

The notion of "classical" may be somewhat confusing, insofar as this term usually refers to the era of classical antiquity in European history. While many discoveries within the mathematics of antiquity remain in full force today, and of the greatest use, the same cannot be said about its "science." This in no way belittles the many important developments, especially within technology, which took place in antiquity and during the Middle Ages in Europe and elsewhere.

The emergence of classical mechanics was a decisive stage in the development of science, in the modern sense of the term. What characterizes it, above all, is its insistence on mathematics (rather than speculation), and its reliance on experiment (rather than observation). With classical mechanics it was established how to formulate quantitative predictions in theory, and how to test them by carefully designed measurement. This provided for much closer scrutiny and testing, both of theory and experiment. This was, and remains, a key factor in establishing certain knowledge, and in bringing it to the service of society. History shows how closely the health and wealth of a society depends on nurturing this investigative and critical approach.

The initial stage in the development of classical mechanics is often referred to as Newtonian Mechanics, and is characterized by the mathematical methods invented by Newton himself, in parallel with Leibniz, and others.

Classical mechanics produces very accurate results within the domain of everyday experience. It is enhanced by Special Relativity for objects moving with large velocity, near the speed of light. Classical mechanics is used to describe the motion of human-sized objects, from projectiles to parts of machinery, as well as astronomical objects, such as spacecraft, planets, stars, and galaxies, and even microscopic objects such as large molecules. Besides this, many specialties exist, dealing with gases, liquids, and solids, and so on. It is one of the largest subjects in science and technology.

Although classical mechanics is largely compatible with other "classical" theories such as classical electrodynamics and thermodynamics, some difficulties were discovered in the late 19th century that can only be resolved by more modern physics. The effort at resolving these problems led to the development of Quantum Mechanics.

Coherence is a property of waves that measures the ability of the waves to interfere with each other. Two waves that are coherent can be combined to produce an unmoving distribution of constructive and destructive interference (a visible *interference pattern*) depending on the relative phase of the waves at their meeting point. (See also **Quantum Coherence** and **Quantum Decoherence**).

Conformation (Chemical) One of the spatial arrangements of atoms in a molecule that can come about through free rotation of the atoms about a single chemical bond.[2]

Consciousness is notoriously difficult to define or locate. Many cultures and religious traditions place the seat of consciousness in a soul separate from the body. Conversely, many scientists and philosophers consider consciousness to be intimately linked to the neural functioning of the brain.

Copenhagen Interpretation (of Quantum Mechanics) is an interpretation of quantum mechanics formulated by Niels Bohr and Werner Heisenberg while collaborating in Copenhagen around 1927. Bohr and Heisenberg extended the probabilistic interpretation of the wavefunction, proposed by Max Born. Their interpretation attempts to answer some perplexing questions, which arise as a result of the wave-particle duality in quantum mechanics, such as the measurement problem.

According to a poll at a Quantum Mechanics workshop in 1997, the Copenhagen interpretation is the most widely accepted specific interpretation of quantum mechanics, followed by the Many Worlds Interpretation. Although current trends show substantial competition from Alternative Interpretations, throughout much of the 20th century the Copenhagen interpretation has had obvious majority acceptance among physicists.

The Copenhagen interpretation assumes that there are two processes influencing the wavefunction: the unitary evolution according to the Schrödinger Equation and the process of the measurement.

While there is no ambiguity about the former, the latter admits several interpretations, even within the Copenhagen interpretation itself. One can either view the wavefunction as a real object that undergoes the wavefunction collapse in the second stage, or one can imagine that the wavefunction is an auxiliary mathematical tool (not a real physical entity) whose only physical meaning is our ability to calculate the probabilities. (See also **Measurement Problem**, **Many Worlds Interpretation**, **Schrödinger Equation** and **Wavefunction Collapse**).

Dendrite is a slender, typically branched projection of a nerve cell, or "neuron," which conducts the electrical stimulation received from other cells to the body or soma of the cell from which it projects. This stimulation arrives through synapses, which typically are located near the tips of the dendrites and away from the soma.

Determinism is the philosophical conception which claims that every physical event, including human cognition and action, is causally determined by an unbroken chain of prior occurrences. No mysterious miracles or totally random events occur.

The principal consequence of deterministic philosophy is that free will (except as defined in strict compatibilism) becomes an illusion. It is a popular misconception that determinism necessarily entails that all future events have already been determined (a position known as Fatalism); this is not obviously the case, and the subject is still debated among metaphysicians. Determinism is associated with, and relies upon, the ideas of Materialism and Causality. Some of the philosophers who have dealt with this issue are Omar Khayyam, David Hume, Thomas Hobbes, Immanuel Kant, and, more recently, John Searle. (See also

Causal Determinism, **Causality** and **Materialism**).

Electron is a subatomic particle. In an atom the electrons surround the nucleus of protons and neutrons in an electron configuration.

Empiricism (Greek [εμπειρισμὸς] "empirical," Latin *experientia*, "experience") is generally regarded as being at the heart of the modern scientific method, that our theories should be based on our observations of the world rather than on intuition or faith; that is, empirical research and a posteriori inductive reasoning rather than purely deductive logic.

Empiricism is contrasted with continental rationalism, epitomized by René Descartes. According to the rationalist, philosophy should be performed via introspection and a priori deductive reasoning. Names associated with empiricism include St. Thomas Aquinas, Aristotle, Thomas Hobbes, Francis Bacon, John Locke, George Berkeley, and David Hume.

Entanglement (See **Quantum Entanglement**)

Esalen Institute is a workshop and retreat center in Big Sur, California. It is considered to be the center of the Human potential movement.

Its website states: "The Esalen Institute was founded by Michael Murphy and Dick Price in 1962 as an alternative educational center devoted to the exploration of what Aldous Huxley called the 'human potential,' the world of unrealized human capacities that lies beyond the imagination. Esalen soon became known for its blend of East/West philosophies, its experiential/ didactic workshops, the steady influx of philosophers, psychologists, artists, and religious thinkers, and its breathtaking grounds blessed with natural hot springs. Once home to a Native American tribe known as the Esselen, Esalen is situated on 27 acres (109,000 m²) of spectacular Big Sur coastline with the Santa Lucia Mountains rising sharply behind." (See also **Human Potential Movement** and **Transpersonal Psychology).**

Fourier Transform, named after Jean Baptiste Joseph Fourier, is an integral transform that re-expresses a function in terms of sinusoidal basis functions, i.e. as a sum or integral of sinusoidal functions multiplied by some coefficients ("amplitudes"). There are many closely related variations of this transform, depending upon the type of function being transformed.

Fourier transforms have many scientific applications — in physics, number theory, signal processing, probability theory, statistics, cryptography, acoustics, oceanography, optics, geometry, and other areas. (In signal processing and related fields, the Fourier transform is typically thought of as decomposing a signal into its component frequencies and their amplitudes.)

Glial Cells or *glia* are non-neuronal cells that provide support and nutrition, maintain homeostasis, form myelin, and participate in signal transmission in the nervous system. In the human brain, glia are estimated to outnumber neurons by as much as 50 to 1.

Heisenberg Uncertainty Principle expresses a limitation on accuracy of (nearly) simultaneous measurement of observables such as the position and the momentum of a particle. It furthermore precisely quantifies the imprecision by providing a lower bound (greater than zero) for the product of the dispersions of the measurements.

Hilbert Space is an inner product space that is complete with respect to the norm defined by the inner product. Hilbert spaces serve to clarify and generalize the concept of Fourier expansion and certain linear transformations such as the Fourier transform. Hilbert spaces are of crucial importance in the mathematical formulation of quantum mechanics, although many basic features of quantum mechanics can be understood without going into details about Hilbert spaces.

Hormone (from Greek *horman*, "to set in motion") is a chemical messenger from one cell (or group of cells) to another. All multicellular organisms (including plants) produce hormones. The best-known hormones are those produced by endocrine glands of vertebrate animals, but nearly every organ system and tissue type in a human or animal body produces hormones. Hormone molecules are secreted (released) directly into the bloodstream, other body fluids, or into adjacent tissues. They move by circulation or diffusion to their target cells, which may be nearby cells (paracrine action) in the same tissue or cells of a distant organ of the body. The function of hormones is to serve as a signal to the target cells; the action of hormones is determined by the pattern of secretion and the signal transduction of the receiving tissue.

Hormone actions vary widely, but can include stimulation or inhibition of growth, induction or suppression of apoptosis (programmed cell death), activation or inhibition of the immune system, regulating metabolism and preparation for a new activity (e.g. fighting, fleeing, mating) or phase of life (e.g. puberty, caring for offspring, menopause). In many cases, one hormone may regulate the production and release of other hormones. Many of the responses to hormone signals can be described as serving to regulate metabolic activity of an organ or tissue. Hormones also control the reproductive cycle of virtually all multicellular organisms.

Humanism A cultural and intellectual movement of the Renaissance that emphasized secular concerns as a result of the rediscovery and study of the literature, art, and civilization of ancient Greece and Rome. (See also **Secular Humanism**).[3]

Human Potential Movement came out of the social and intellectual milieu of the 1960s and was formed to promote the cultivation of extraordinary potential believed to be largely untapped in most people. The movement is premised on the belief that through the development of largely untapped potential for extraordinary capabilities, humans can experience an exceptional quality of life filled with happiness, creativity, and fulfillment. A corollary belief is that those who begin to unleash this potential will find their actions within society to be directed towards helping others release their potential. The belief is that the net effect of individuals cultivating their potential will bring about positive social change at large.

The movement has its conceptual roots in existentialism and humanism. Its formation was strongly tied to Humanistic Psychology, also known as the "3rd force" in psychology (after psychoanalysis and behaviorism, and before the "4th force" of Transpersonal Psychology which emphasizes psychic, mystical, and spiritual development). It is often considered synonymous with Humanistic psychology. The movement views Abraham Maslow's idea of self-actualization as the supreme expression of a human's life. (See also **Esalen Institute**, **Humanism** and **Transpersonal Psychology**).

Huxley, Aldous (1894-1963) was a British writer who

emigrated to the United States. He was a member of the famous Huxley family who produced a number of brilliant scientific minds. Best known for his novels and wide-ranging output of essays, he also published short stories, poetry, and travel writing. Through his novels and essays, Huxley functioned as an examiner and sometimes critic of social morés, societal norms and ideals, and possible misapplications of science in human life. While his earlier concerns might be called "humanist," ultimately, he became quite interested in "spiritual" subjects like parapsychology and mystically based philosophy, which he also wrote about. By the end of his life, Huxley was considered, in certain learned circles, a "leader of modern thought."

Idealism In philosophy, idealism is any theory positing the primacy of spirit, mind, or language over matter. It includes claiming that thought has some crucial role in making the world the way it is; that thought and the world are made for one another, or that they make one another.

Lemuria is the name given by 19th century geologist Philip Sclater to a hypothetical landmass in the Indian Ocean that was required, before the understanding of plate tectonics, to account for similarities between fauna in India and Madagascar. The name derived from the lemurs that are endemic to Madagascar.

Its 19th century origins lie in the geological theory of catastrophism, but since then it has been adopted by Occult writers, as well as the Tamil people of India as the name of a Lost Land variously located in the Indian and Pacific Oceans.

Accounts of Lemuria differ regarding most of its specifics. However, all share a common belief that the continent existed in pre-history but sank beneath the ocean as a result of geological change.

Scientists today regard sunken continents as physical impossibilities.

Ligand comes from the Latin *ligare*, "that which binds" (from the same root as *religion*). Any of a variety of small molecules that specifically bind a cellular receptor and in so doing convey an information message to the cell.[4]

Macroscopic means measurable and observable by the naked eye; describes existence, as we perceive it.

Magic (from the Magi: Old Persian *Magupati*, Persian *Mobed*, Greek [Μάγοι]) is a term referring to the influence of events and physical phenomena through supernatural, mystical, or paranormal means. The term *magic* in its various translations has been used in a number of ways. From the point of view of an established religion, it has often been used as a pejorative term for the pagan rituals of competing ethnic groups, as belonging to an inferior (hence blasphemous or idolatrous) culture.

Among occultists, magic is a fairly neutral term which has some varied connotations, such as *white magic* and *black magic*. The famous occultist Aleister Crowley chose the spelling magick to distinguish "the true science of the Magi from all its "counterfeits," such as stage magic. Today many use that spelling in the same or otherwise similar way, often to connote a pagan or wiccan system of belief rituals, that endow individuals with superphysical abilities.

As with all paranormal claims, magic has as yet failed to be supported by credible controlled scientific experimentation and can only be studied seriously for its influence in cultural or religious matters.

Magick is an alternate spelling of magic, coined by Aleister Crowley to differentiate 'the true science of the Magi from all its counterfeits'. Although it is widely believed that this meant distinguishing genuine magic from stage magic, there is no evidence that Crowley intended this interpretation. Crowley got the inspiration for the spelling from its usage by the famous Elizabethan magician John Dee.

Crowley defined magick as "the science and art of causing change to occur in conformity with the will." By this, he included mundane acts of will as well as ritual magic.

Concentration or meditation plays an important role in Crowley's system. A certain amount of restricting the mind to some imagined object, according to this theory, produces mystical attainment or "an occurrence in the brain characterized essentially by the uniting of subject and object." (Book Four, Part 1: Mysticism)

Magick, as defined previously, seeks to aid concentration by constantly recalling the attention to the chosen object (or Will), thereby producing said attainment. For example, if one wishes to concentrate on a god, one might memorize a system of correspondences (perhaps chosen arbitrarily, as this would not affect its usefulness for mystical purposes) and then make every object that one sees "correspond" to said god.

Many Worlds Interpretation of Quantum Mechanics (or MWI) is an interpretation of quantum mechanics that averts the special role played by the measurement process in the Copenhagen Interpretation by proposing several key ideas. The first of these is the existence of a state function for the entire universe, which obeys Schrödinger's Equation for all time. The second idea is that the universal state is a quantum superposition of an infinite number of states of identical non-communicating "parallel universes." The ideas of MWI originated in Hugh Everett's Princeton Ph.D. thesis, but the phrase "many worlds" is due to Bryce DeWitt, who wrote more on the topic of Everett's original work. DeWitt's formulation has become so popular that many confuse it with Everett's original work.

As with the other interpretations of quantum mechanics, the Many Worlds Interpretation is motivated by behavior that can be illustrated by the double-slit experiment. When particles of light (or anything else) are passed through the double slit, a calculation assuming wave-like behavior of light is needed to identify where the particles are likely to be observed. Yet when the particles are observed, they appear as particles and not as non-localized waves. The Copenhagen Interpretation of quantum mechanics proposed a process of "collapse" from wave behavior to particle-like behavior to explain this phenomenon of observation. (See also **Copenhagen Interpretation** and **Schrödinger's Equation**).

Materialism is the philosophical view that the only thing that can truly be said to "exist" is matter; that fundamentally, all things are comprised of "material." Materialism has also frequently been understood to designate an entire scientific, "rationalistic" worldview, particularly by religious thinkers opposed to it and also by Marxists. It typically contrasts with dualism and idealism, among others.

Measurement Problem is the key set of questions that every interpretation of quantum mechanics must answer. The problem is that the wavefunction in quantum mechanics evolves according to the Schrödinger Equation into a linear superposition of different states but the actual measurements always find the physical system in a definite state. (See also **Schrödinger's Equation, Superposition** and **Wavefunction Collapse**).

Metaphysics 1. The branch of philosophy that examines the nature of reality, including the relationship between mind and matter, substance and attribute, fact and value. 2. (*used with a pl. verb*) The theoretical or first principles of a particular discipline: *the metaphysics of law*. 3. (*used with a sing. verb*) A priori speculation upon questions that are unanswerable to scientific observation, analysis, or experiment. 4. (*used with a sing. verb*) Excessively subtle or recondite reasoning.[5]

Microtubules are protein structures found within cells. They have diameter of ~ 24 nm and varying length from several micrometers to possible millimeters in axons of nerve cells. Microtubules are polymers of tubulin. They are hollow cylinders, which can be thought of as 13 protofilaments of tubulin arranged into a cylinder, or as a single spiral with 13 subunits in one helical turn of the spiral. Microtubules have a polarity: each microtubule has a (+) and a (-) end. Gain or loss of tubulin subunits from the (+) end can change the length of a microtubule.

Microtubules are part of a structural network (the cytoskeleton) within the cell's cytoplasm, but in addition to structural support microtubules are used in many other processes as well. They are capable of growing and shrinking in order to generate force, and there are also motor proteins that move along the microtubule. A notable structure involving microtubules is the mitotic spindle used by cells to segregate their chromosomes correctly during cell division.

Monism is the metaphysical position that all is of one

essential essence, substance or energy. Monism is to be distinguished from dualism, which holds that ultimately there are two kinds of substance, and from pluralism, which holds that ultimately there are many kinds of substance.

Monotheism The doctrine or belief that there is only one God.

Mysticism (ancient Greek *mysticon* = secret) is meditation, prayer, or theology focused on the direct experience of union with divinity, God, or Ultimate Reality; or the belief that such experience is a genuine and important source of knowledge.

Neurons or nerve cells; the primary cells of the nervous system. In vertebrates, they are found in the brain, the spinal cord and in the nerves and ganglia of the peripheral nervous system.

Neuropeptide Any of the nearly 100 small peptide informational substances initially described as neuronal secretions. More recent observations that lymphocytes and monocytes both secrete and respond to neuropeptides has, of course, rendered this term somewhat inaccurate, and immunologists favor terms like cytokine, or chemokine, but neuroscientists still commonly refer to neuropeptides.[6]

Neurotransmitter A chemical that relays, amplifies and modulates electrical signals between two neurons: the presynaptic neuron and the postsynaptic neuron.

Neutron In physics, the neutron is a subatomic particle with no net electric charge and a mass of 939.6 MeV/c^2 (1.6749

$\times 10^{-27}$ kg, slightly more than a proton). Its spin is ½.

The nucleus of most atoms (all except the most common isotope of hydrogen, which consists of a single proton only) consists of protons and neutrons.

New Age Movement describes a broad movement in Western culture characterized by an individual eclectic approach to spiritual exploration. It has some attributes of a new, emerging religion but is currently a loose network of spiritual seekers, teachers, healers and other participants. The name "New Age" also refers to the market segment in which goods and services are sold to people in the movement.

Rather than follow the lead of an organized religion, "New Agers" typically construct their own spiritual journey based on material taken as needed from mystical traditions from all over the world, as well as shamanism, neopaganism and occultism. Participants are likely to dip into many diverse teachings and practices, some mainstream and some fringe, and formulate their own beliefs and practices based on their experiences in each. No clear membership or rigid boundaries actually exist. The movement is most visible where its ideas are traded, for example in alternative bookstores, music stores, and fairs.

Most New Age activity may be characterized as a form of alternative spirituality. Even apparent exceptions (such as alternative health practices) often turn out to have some spiritual dimension (for example, the integration of mind, body, and spirit). "Alternative" here means, with respect to the dominant Western Judeo-Christian culture. It is no accident that most New Age ideas and practices seem to contain implicit critiques of mainstream Christianity in particular. An emphasis on meditation suggests that ordinary prayer is insufficient;

belief in reincarnation (which not all New Agers accept) challenges familiar Christian doctrines of the afterlife.

Newtonian Physics (See **Classical Mechanics**).

Noetic Sciences (Institute of) Founded in 1973 by astronaut Edgar Mitchell, the Institute of Noetic Sciences explores the frontiers of consciousness through rigorous scientific research, bridges science and spirit, and seeks to support a fundamental shift in human consciousness to create a world grounded in freedom, wisdom and love. The Institute publishes a quarterly review call *Shift: At the Frontiers of Consciousness*. It is a membership organization with 30,000 members worldwide. The headquarters are in Petaluma, California, on a 200-acre (0.8 km²) campus, which houses an active retreat and learning center.

Among the projects it has sponsored are a comprehensive bibliography on the physical and psychological effects of meditation, an extensive spontaneous remission bibliography, and studies on the efficacy of compassionate intention on healing in AIDS patients. Current research and education is focused on three primary areas: Extended Human Capacities, Integral Health & Healing, and Emerging Worldviews.

Non-Locality in quantum mechanics, refers to the property of entangled quantum states in which both the entangled states "collapse" *simultaneously* upon measurement of one of their entangled components, regardless of the spatial separation of the two states. (See also **Quantum Entanglement**).

Objective Reduction/Subjective Reduction or Orchestrated Objective Reduction ("Orch OR") Superpositioned states each have their own space-time geometries. When the degree of coherent mass-energy difference leads to sufficient separation of space-time geometry, the system must choose and decay (reduce, [i.e., wavefunction] collapse) to a single universe state. In this way, a transient superposition of slightly differing space-time geometries persists until an abrupt quantum classical reduction occurs. Unlike the random, "*subjective reduction*" (SR, or R) of standard quantum theory caused by observation or environmental entanglement, the OR we propose in microtubules is a self-collapse and it results in particular patterns of microtubule-tubulin conformational states that regulate neuronal activities including synaptic functions.[7] (See also **Conformation** and **Wavefunction Collapse**).

Observer In general, an observer is any system which receives information from an object.

Observer Created Reality (See **Observer Effect**).

Observer Effect is the term for how someone observing and measuring an effect can change the thing being observed.

In quantum mechanics, if the outcome of an event has not been observed, it exists in a state of superposition, which is being in all possible states at once. The most famous example is the thought experiment Schrödinger's cat, in which the cat is neither alive nor dead until observed — until that time, the cat is both alive and dead.

Peptide any of various natural or synthetic compounds containing two or more amino acids linked by the carboxyl group of one amino acid and the amino group of another.[8]

Physics (from the Greek, [φυσικός] (*phusikos*), "natural," and [φύσις] (*phusis*), "nature") is the science of nature in the broadest sense. Physicists study the behavior and properties of matter in a wide variety of contexts, ranging from the sub-nuclear particles from which all ordinary matter is made (particle physics) to the behavior of the material Universe as a whole (cosmology).

Some of the properties studied in physics are common to *all* material systems, such as the conservation of energy. Such properties are often referred to as laws of physics. Physics is sometimes said to be the "fundamental science," because each of the other natural sciences (biology, chemistry, geology, etc.) deals with particular types of material systems that obey the laws of physics. For example, chemistry is the science of molecules and the chemicals that they form in the bulk. The properties of a chemical are determined by the properties of the underlying molecules, which are accurately described by areas of physics such as quantum mechanics, thermodynamics, and electromagnetism.

Physics is also closely related to mathematics. Physical theories are almost invariably expressed using mathematical relations, and the mathematics involved is generally more complicated than in the other sciences. The difference between physics and mathematics is that physics is ultimately concerned with descriptions of the material world, whereas mathematics is concerned with abstract patterns that need not have any bearing on it.

Planck's Constant is a physical constant that is used to describe the sizes of quanta. It plays a central role in the theory of quantum mechanics, and is named after Max Planck, one of the founders of quantum theory.

Protein (in Greek [πρωτέϊνη] = *first element*) is a complex, high molecular weight organic compound that consists of amino acids joined by peptide bonds. Proteins are essential to the structure and function of all living cells and viruses. Many proteins are enzymes or subunits of enzymes. Other proteins play structural or mechanical roles, such as those that form the struts and joints of the cytoskeleton. Still more functions filled by proteins include immune response and the storage and transport of various ligands. In nutrition, proteins serve as the source of amino acids for organisms that do not synthesize those amino acids natively.

Proteins are one of the classes of bio-macromolecules, alongside polysaccharides and nucleic acids that make up the primary constituents of living things. They are amongst the most actively studied molecule in biochemistry and were discovered by Jöns Jakob Berzelius, in 1838.

Proton In physics, the proton (Greek *proton* = first) is a subatomic particle with an electric charge of one positive fundamental unit (1.602×10^{-19} coulomb) and a mass of 938.3 MeV/$c2$ (1.6726×10^{-27} kg, or about 1836 times the mass of an electron).

Pseudoscience is any body of knowledge purported to be scientific or supported by science but which is judged by the mainstream scientific community to fail to comply with the scientific method. Pseudoscience is seen as a kind of counterfeit or masquerade of science that makes use of some of the superficial trappings of science but does not involve the substance of science.

The possibility of separating out "scientific" from "non-scientific" practices on the basis of methodological distinctions is highly contested in the philosophical and historical community (see "the problem of demarcation," below). As the term pseudoscience has negative connotations, those who are labeled as practicing or advocating it almost always reject this classification, and often the distinction itself.

Some critics of pseudoscience consider some or all forms of pseudoscience to be harmless entertainment. Others, such as Richard Dawkins, consider all forms of pseudoscience to be harmful, whether or not they result in immediate harm to their followers. These critics generally consider that advocacy of pseudoscience may occur for a number of reasons, ranging from simple naïveté about the nature of science and the scientific method, to deliberate deception for financial or political benefit.

Quantum Coherence is a state of balance when the individual frequencies of two or more quanta are in constructive interaction (See also **Coherence**).

Quantum Computer is any device for computation that makes direct use of distinctively quantum mechanical phenomena, such as superposition and entanglement, to perform operations on data. In a classical (or conventional) computer, data are measured by bits; in a quantum computer the data are measured by qubits. The basic principle of quantum computation is that the quantum properties of particles can be used to represent and structure data, and that devised quantum mechanisms can be used to perform operations with these data.

Quantum Cryptography is an approach to securing communications based on certain phenomena of quantum physics. Unlike traditional cryptography, which employs various mathematical techniques to restrict eavesdroppers from learning the contents of encrypted messages, quantum cryptography is focused on the physics of information. The process of sending and storing information is always carried out by physical means, for example photons in optical fibers or electrons in electric current. Eavesdropping can be viewed as measurements on a physical object, in this case the carrier of the information. What the eavesdropper can measure, and how, depends exclusively on the laws of physics. Using quantum phenomena such as quantum superpositions or quantum entanglement one can design and implement a communication system, which can always detect eavesdropping. This is because measurements on the quantum carrier of information disturb it and so leave traces.

Some commercially available products have appeared based on quantum cryptography, for example, *ID Quantique* or *MagiQ*.

Quantum Decoherence In quantum mechanics, quantum decoherence is the general term for the consequences of irreversible quantum entanglement. These processes typically change the behavior of a system from quantum mechanical to classical. Decoherence is always present when a system is interacting with other systems and thereby to be viewed as an open system.

The effect is basically one in which the system under consideration loses the phase coherence between certain components of its quantum mechanical state and hence no longer exhibits the essentially quantum properties (such as superposition and entanglement) associated with such coherence. In an idealized situation, the states of the other system (usually called "the environment") change according to the system states, as in a measurement. The ensuing entanglement delocalizes quantum coherences to the combined system. As a consequence, the system appears to be in a "mixed state," i.e., it shows the same properties as an ensemble of certain states without any coherence between them.

Decoherence represents an extremely fast process for macroscopic objects, since these are interacting with many microscopic objects in their natural environment. The process explains why we tend not to observe quantum behavior in everyday macroscopic objects since these exist in a bath of air molecules and photons. It also explains why we do see classical fields from the properties of the interaction between matter and radiation.

Quantum Entanglement is a quantum mechanical phenomenon in which the quantum states of two or more objects have to be described with reference to each other, even though the individual objects may be spatially separated. This leads to correlations between observable physical properties of the systems. For example, it is possible to prepare two particles in a single quantum state such that when one is observed to be spin-up, the other one will always be observed to be spin-down and vice versa, this despite the fact that it is impossible to predict, according to quantum mechanics, which set of measurements will be observed. As a result, measurements performed on one system seem to be instantaneously influencing other systems entangled with it. However, classical information cannot be transmitted through entanglement faster than the speed of light.

Quantum entanglement is the basis for emerging technologies such as quantum computing and quantum cryptography, and has been used for experiments in quantum teleportation. At the same time, it produces some of the more theoretically and philosophically disturbing aspects of the theory, as one can show that the correlations predicted by quantum mechanics are inconsistent with the seemingly obvious principle of local realism, which is that information about the state of a system should only be mediated by interactions in its immediate surroundings. Different views of what is actually occurring in the process of quantum entanglement give rise to different interpretations of quantum mechanics.

Quantum Field Theory (QFT) is the application of quantum mechanics to fields. It provides a theoretical framework widely used in particle physics and condensed matter physics. This framework is necessary in order to formulate consistent relativistic quantum theories, such as quantum electrodynamics, the quantum theory of electromagnetism, one of the most well-tested and successful theories in physics. However, not all quantum field theories are relativistic; the BCS theory is an example of a non-relativistic quantum field theory, which has been highly successful in describing superconductivity.

The fundamentals of quantum field theory were developed between the late 1920s and the 1950s, notably by Dirac, Fock, Pauli, Tomonaga, Schwinger, Feynman and Dyson.

Quantum Gravity is the field of theoretical physics attempting to unify the theory of quantum mechanics, which describes three of the fundamental forces of nature, with general relativity, the theory of the fourth fundamental force: gravity. The ultimate goal of some (e.g. string theory) is a unified framework for all fundamental forces — a theory of everything.

Quantum Mechanics is a fundamental physical theory, which extends and corrects Newtonian mechanics, especially at the atomic and subatomic levels. It is the underlying framework of many fields of physics and chemistry, including condensed matter physics, quantum chemistry, and particle physics. The term *quantum* (Latin for how much) refers to the discrete units that the theory assigns to certain physical quantities, such as the energy of an atom at rest.

Quantum mechanics is a theory of mechanics, a branch of physics that deals with the motion of bodies and associated physical quantities such as energy and momentum. It is believed to be a more fundamental theory than Newtonian Mechanics, because it provides accurate and precise descriptions for many phenomena where Newtonian mechanics drastically fails. This includes the behavior of systems at atomic length scales and below (in fact, Newtonian mechanics is unable to account for the existence of stable atoms), as well as special macroscopic systems such as superconductors and superfluids. The predictions of quantum mechanics have never been disproved after a century's worth of experiments.

Quantum mechanics incorporates at least three classes of phenomena that classical physics cannot account for: (i) the quantization (discretization) of certain physical quantities, (ii) wave-particle duality, and (iii) quantum entanglement.

Quantum Teleportation is a technique discussed in quantum information science to transfer a quantum state to an arbitrarily distant location using an entangled state and the transmission of some classical information.

Quantum Tunneling is the quantum-mechanical effect of transitioning through a classically forbidden energy state. The often-repeated analogy would be if a roller coaster car were to make it up and over a hill when it did not have enough kinetic energy to surmount it, according to classical mechanics.

One of its major applications is in electron-tunneling

microscopes, which are used to see objects too small to be seen using conventional microscopes. Electron tunneling microscopes overcome the limiting effects of conventional microscopes, such as optical aberrations and wavelength limitations by scanning the surface of an object with tunneling electrons.

Rama is a Hindu incarnation of God, said to be one of the ten avatars (incarnations/bodily manifestations of God) of Vishnu (the second aspect of God in the Hindu trinity; he is considered *"the preserver"*). There is debate, existing mainly in the Western countries, as to whether he was a real or mythical king in ancient India. In Eastern countries, he is largely regarded as real. His life and heroic deeds are related in the Hindu Sanskrit epic the *Ramayana*.

The spelling and pronunciation of *Rama* follows the original Sanskrit; it continues to be followed in several modern languages of India. In modern Indian vernaculars, however, it is sometimes pronounced as "Ram."

Rama is the embodiment of the absolute — Brahman. There is debate to whether Shri Rama was aware of his own divinity during his years in human form. One purpose of his incarnation was to carry out leadership by example. He exemplifies the perfect man through his proper conduct regardless of the unfavorableness of circumstance.

Astronomical data in the *Ramayana* has been interpreted to suggest that his reign would have been at approximately 2015 BCE but more conservative estimates place the writing at anywhere from around 1500 BCE to 500 BCE. The *Ramayana* is a great literary work and piece of devotional and philosophical literature revered by both Hindus and individuals of other cultures.

Rationalism is a philosophical doctrine that asserts that the truth should be determined by reason and factual analysis, rather than faith, dogma or religious teaching.

Outside of religious discussion, the discipline of rationalism may be applied more generally, for example to political or social issues. In these cases it is the rejection of emotion, tradition or fashionable belief, which is the defining feature of the rationalist perspective.

Receptor is a protein on the cell membrane or within the cytoplasm or cell nucleus that binds to a specific factor (a ligand), such as a neurotransmitter, hormone, or other substance, and initiates the cellular response to the ligand. As all receptors are proteins, their structure is encoded into the DNA. Most hormone genes contain a short sequence that signals to the cell whether it needs to be transported to the cell membrane or it is to remain in the cytoplasm. (See also **Hormone**, **Ligand**, **Neuropeptide**, **Neurotransmitter** and **Peptide**).

Relativity (General Theory of) is a fundamental physical theory of gravitation, which corrects and extends Newtonian gravitation, especially at the macroscopic level of stars or planets.

General relativity may be regarded as an extension of Special Relativity, this latter theory correcting Newtonian Mechanics at high velocities. General relativity has a unique role amongst physical theories in the sense that it interprets the gravitational field as a geometric phenomenon. More specifically, it assumes that any object possessing mass curves the "space" in which it exists, this curvature being equated to gravity. To conceptualize this equivalence, it is helpful think to of it, as several author-physicists have suggested, in terms of gravity not causing or being caused by spacetime curvature, but rather that gravity IS spacetime curvature. It deals with the motion of bodies in such "curved spaces" and has survived every experimental test performed on it since its formulation by Albert Einstein in 1915.

General relativity forms the basis for modern studies in fields such as astronomy, cosmology and astrophysics. It describes with great accuracy and precision many phenomena where classical physics (a.k.a. Newtonian) fails, such as the perihelion motion of planets (classical physics cannot fully account for the perihelion shift of Mercury, for example) and the bending of starlight by the Sun (again, classical physics can only account for half the experimentally observed bending). It also predicts phenomena such as the existence of gravitational waves, black holes and the expansion of the universe.

Unlike the other revolutionary physical theory, quantum mechanics, General Relativity was essentially formulated by one man, Albert Einstein. However, Einstein required the help of one of his friends, Marcel Grossmann, to help him with the mathematics of General Relativity.

Relativity (Special Theory of) is the physical theory published in 1905 by Albert Einstein. It replaced Newtonian notions of space and time and incorporated electromagnetism as represented by Maxwell's equations. The theory is called "special" because it is a special case of Einstein's principle of relativity where the effects of gravity can be ignored. Ten years later, Einstein published the theory of General Relativity, which incorporates gravitation.

Schrödinger Equation, proposed by the Austrian physicist, Erwin Schrödinger in 1925, describes the time-dependence of quantum mechanical systems. It is of central importance to the theory of quantum mechanics, playing a role analogous to Newton's

Second Law in Classical Mechanics.

In the mathematical formulation of quantum mechanics, each system is associated with a complex Hilbert Space such that each instantaneous state of the system is described by a unit vector in that space. This state vector encodes the probabilities for the outcomes of all possible measurements applied to the system. As the state of a system generally changes over time, the state vector is a function of time. The Schrödinger equation provides a quantitative description of the rate of change of the state vector.

Science a. The observation, identification, description, experimental investigation, and theoretical explanation of phenomena. **b.** Such activities restricted to a class of natural phenomena. **c.** Such activities applied to an object of inquiry or study.[9]

Secular Humanism An outlook or philosophy that advocates human rather than religious values.[10]

Self-Actualization (a term originated by Kurt Goldstein) is the instinctual need of a human to make the most of their unique abilities. Maslow described it as follows:

A musician must make music, the artist must paint, a poet must write, if he is to be ultimately at peace with himself. What a man can be, he must be. This need we may call self-actualization. (Motivation and Personality, 1954.)

Maslow writes of self-actualizing people that:

- They embrace the facts and realities of the world (including themselves) rather than denying or avoiding them.
- They are spontaneous in their ideas and actions.
- They are creative.
- They are interested in solving problems; this often includes the problems of others. Solving these problems

is often a key focus in their lives.
- They feel a closeness to other people, and generally appreciate life.
- They have a system of morality that is fully internalized and independent of external authority.
- They judge others without prejudice, in a way that can be termed *objective*.

Skepticism can mean:
- Philosophical skepticism: a philosophical position in which people choose to critically examine whether the knowledge and perceptions that they have are actually true, and whether or not one can ever be said to have absolutely true knowledge; or
- Scientific skepticism: a scientific, or practical, position in which one questions the veracity of claims, and seeks to prove or disprove them using the scientific method.

Spiritualism A philosophy, doctrine, or religion emphasizing the spiritual aspect of being.[11]

Steroids are fat-soluble (lipid) organic compounds that occur naturally throughout the plant and animal kingdoms and play important functional roles. Steroids are quite diverse and include molecules like cholesterol, all sex hormones, and the adrenal cortical hormones (corticosteroids). Sex hormones are necessary for many aspects of reproduction and sexual function, while adrenocortical hormones primarily affect carbohydrate and protein metabolism. The hormonal steroids act via receptors located not on the surface of the cell but deep within, in the nucleus, where they regulate the transcription of various genes. In this respect, they differ from the neurotransmitters and peptide informational substances that act rapidly on receptors at the cell surface.[12]

Supernatural 1. Of or relating to existence outside the natural world. **2.** Attributed to a power that seems to violate or go beyond natural forces. **3.** Of or relating to a deity. **4.** Of or relating to the immediate exercise of divine power; miraculous. **5.** Of or relating to the miraculous.

Superposition occurs when an object simultaneously "possesses" two or more values for an observable quantity (e.g. the position or energy of a particle).

Synapses are specialized junctions through which cells of the nervous system signal to one another and to non-neuronal cells such as muscles or glands.

Synapses form the circuits in which the neurons of the central nervous system interconnect. They are thus crucial to the biological computations that underlie perception and thought. They also provide the means through which the nervous system connects to and controls the other systems of the body.

The word "synapse" comes from "synaptein" which Sir Charles Scott Sherrington and his colleagues coined from the Greek "syn-" meaning "together" and "haptein" meaning "to clasp."

Theory of Everything is a theory of theoretical physics and mathematics that fully explains and links together all known physical phenomena (i.e. "everything"). Initially the term was used with an ironical connotation, to refer to various overgeneralized theories. Over time, the term stuck in popularizations of quantum physics to describe a theory that would unify the theories of the four fundamental interactions of nature, possibly due to the influence of *The Theory of Everything*, a book with material written by Stephen Hawking but later disowned by him.

There have been numerous theories of everything proposed by theoretical physicists over the last century, but as yet none has been able to stand up to experimental scrutiny or there is tremendous difficulty in getting the theories to produce even experimentally testable results. The primary problem in producing a theory of everything is that quantum mechanics and general relativity have radically different descriptions of the universe, and the obvious ways of combining the two lead quickly to the renormalization problem in which the theory does not give finite results for experimentally testable quantities. (See also **Unified Field Theory**).

Theosophy is a body of belief, which holds that all religions are attempts by man to ascertain "the Divine," and as such each religion has a portion of the truth. Theosophy, as a coherent belief system, developed from the writings of Helena Petrovna Blavatsky. Together with Henry Steel Olcott, William Quan Judge, and others she founded the Theosophical Society in 1875.

A more formal definition from the *Concise Oxford Dictionary* describes theosophy as "any of various philosophies professing to achieve a knowledge of God by spiritual ecstasy, direct intuition, or special individual relations, esp. a modern movement following Hindu and Buddhist teachings and seeking universal brotherhood."

Adherents of theosophy maintain that it is a "body of truth" that forms the basis of all religions. Theosophy, they claim, represents a modern face of Hinduism's *Sanatana Dharma*, "the Eternal Truth," as the proper religion of man. *Christian Theosophy* is a term used to designate the knowledge of God and of Jesus obtained by the direct intuition of the Divine essence.

The five prominent symbols visible in the Seal of the

Theosophical Society are the Star of David, the Ankh, the Swastika, the Ouroboros, and above the seal is the Aum. Around the seal are written the words: *There is no religion higher than truth.*

Transactional Interpretation of quantum mechanics by Professor John Cramer is an unusual interpretation of quantum mechanics that describes quantum interactions in terms of a standing wave formed by retarded (forward in time) and advanced (backward in time) waves. The author argues that it avoids the philosophical problems with the Copenhagen interpretation and the role of the observer, and elegantly resolves various quantum paradoxes. Fred Alan Wolf bases his ideas about *The Yoga of Time Travel* on Cramer's work.

Transpersonal Psychology is a school of psychology, considered by proponents to be the "fourth force" in the field (after the first three: psychoanalysis, behaviorism, and humanism). It was originally founded in 1969 by Abraham Maslow, Stanislav Grof, Anthony Sutich and others in order to pursue knowledge about issues connected to mystical and transcendent experiences. A major motivating factor behind the initiative to establish this school of psychology was Abraham Maslow's already published work regarding human peak experiences. It was Grof who coined the term "transpersonal psychology," which refers to the psychological study of experiences, which transcend the traditional boundaries of the ego, i.e. which are "transpersonal," or "transegoic."

According to its proponents, the traditional schools of psychology; behaviorism, psychoanalysis and humanism have failed to include these "transegoic" elements of human existence, such as religious conversion, altered states of consciousness and spirituality. Thus, transpersonal psychology strives to combine insights from modern psychology with insights from the world's contemplative traditions, both East and West.

Tubulin is the protein that makes up microtubules. Microtubules are assembled from molecules of α- and β-tubulin.

Unified Field Theory (UFT) is an attempt to unify all the fundamental forces and the interactions between elementary particles into a single theoretical framework. The term was coined by Einstein who attempted to reconcile the general theory of relativity with electromagnetism in a single field theory. His quest proved elusive and a unified field theory, sometimes grandiosely referred to as the Theory of Everything (TOE, for short), has remained the Holy Grail for physicists, the long-sought theory which would explain the nature and behavior of all matter.

In physics, the forces between objects can be described as mediated by fields. Current theory says that at subatomic distances, these fields are replaced by quantum fields interacting according to the laws of quantum mechanics. Alternatively, using the particle-wave duality of quantum mechanics, fields can be described in terms of exchange partcles that transfer momentum and energy between objects. Crudely speaking, objects interact as they emit and absorb exchange particles, in effect playing a subatomic game of "catch." The essential belief of a unified field theory is that the four fundamental forces (see below) as well as all matter are simply different manifestations of a single fundamental field.

A unified field theory aims to reconcile the four fundamental forces (or fields) of nature, namely:
– Strong force: Force responsible for holding quarks

together to form neutrons and protons, and holding neutrons and protons together to form nuclei. The exchange particles that mediate this force are gluons.

– Electromagnetic force: It is the familiar force that acts on electrically charged particle. The photon is the exchange particle for this force.

– Weak force: Responsible for radioactivity, it is a repulsive short-range interaction that acts on electrons, neutrinos and quarks. It is governed by the W boson.

– Gravitational force: A long-range attractive force that acts on all particles. The exchange particles have been postulated and named gravitons.

Wavefunction In Max Born's probabilistic interpretation of the wavefunction, the amplitude squared of the wavefunction $|\psi(x)|^2$ is the probability density of the particle's position.

Wavefunction Collapse In certain interpretations of quantum mechanics, wavefunction collapse is one of two processes by which quantum systems apparently evolve according to the laws of quantum mechanics. The existence of the wavefunction collapse is required in:

– the version of the Copenhagen Interpretation where the wavefunction is real

– the so-called Transactional Interpretation

– in a "spiritual interpretation" in which consciousness causes collapse.

On the other hand, the collapse does not occur in:

– the version of the Copenhagen Interpretation where the wavefunction is not real

– the interpretation based on Consistent Histories

– the Many Worlds Interpretation

– the Bohm Interpretation.

The cluster of phenomena described by the expression

wavefunction collapse is a fundamental problem in the interpretation of quantum mechanics known as the measurement problem. The problem is not really confronted by the Copenhagen Interpretation, which simply postulates that this is a special characteristic of the "measurement" process. The Everett *Many Worlds Interpretation* deals with it by discarding the collapse-process, thus reformulating the relation between measurement apparatus and system in such a way that the linear laws of quantum mechanics are universally valid, that is, the only process according to which a quantum system evolves is governed by the Schrödinger Equation. Often tied in with the many-worlds interpretation but not limited to it is the physical process of decoherence, which causes an *apparent* collapse. Decoherence is also important for the interpretation based on Consistent Histories.

All definitions derived from Wikipedia The Free Encyclopedia, unless otherwise noted.

is a licensee, and is addressed as "you". You accept the license if you copy, modify or distribute the work in a way requiring permission under copyright law.

A "Modified Version" of the Document means any work containing the Document or a portion of it, either copied verbatim, or with modifications and/or translated into another language.

A "Secondary Section" is a named appendix or a front-matter section of the Document that deals exclusively with the relationship of the publishers or authors of the Document to the Document's overall subject (or to related matters) and contains nothing that could fall directly within that overall subject. (Thus, if the Document is in part a textbook of mathematics, a Secondary Section may not explain any mathematics.) The relationship could be a matter of historical connection with the subject or with related matters, or of legal, commercial, philosophical, ethical or political position regarding them.

The "Invariant Sections" are certain Secondary Sections whose titles are designated, as being those of Invariant Sections, in the notice that says that the Document is released under this License. If a section does not fit the above definition of Secondary then it is not allowed to be designated as Invariant. The Document may contain zero Invariant Sections. If the Document does not identify any Invariant Sections then there are none.

The "Cover Texts" are certain short passages of text that are listed, as Front-Cover Texts or Back-Cover Texts, in the notice that says that the Document is released under this License. A Front-Cover Text may be at most 5 words, and a Back-Cover Text may be at most 25 words.

A "Transparent" copy of the Document means a machine-readable copy, represented in a format whose specification is available to the general public, that is suitable for revising the document straightforwardly with generic text editors or (for images composed of pixels) generic paint programs or (for drawings) some widely available drawing editor, and that is suitable for input to text formatters or for automatic translation to a variety of formats suitable for input to text formatters. A copy made in an otherwise Transparent file format whose markup, or absence of markup, has been arranged to thwart or discourage subsequent modification by readers is not Transparent. An image format is not Transparent if used for any substantial amount of text. A copy that is not "Transparent" is called "Opaque".

Examples of suitable formats for Transparent copies include plain ASCII without markup, Texinfo input format, LaTeX input format, SGML or XML using a publicly available DTD, and standard-conforming simple HTML, PostScript or PDF designed for human modification. Examples of transparent image formats include PNG, XCF and JPG. Opaque formats include proprietary formats that can be read and edited only by proprietary word processors, SGML or XML for which the DTD and/or processing tools are not generally available, and the machine-generated HTML, PostScript or PDF produced by some word processors for output purposes only.

The "Title Page" means, for a printed book, the title page itself, plus such following pages as are needed to hold, legibly, the material this License requires to appear in the title page. For works in formats which do not have any title page as such, "Title Page" means the text near the most prominent appearance of the work's title, preceding the beginning of the body of the text.

A section "Entitled XYZ" means a named subunit of the Document whose title either is precisely XYZ or contains XYZ in parentheses following text that translates XYZ in another language. (Here XYZ stands for a specific section name mentioned below, such as "Acknowledgements", "Dedications", "Endorsements", or "History".) To "Preserve the Title" of such a section when you modify the Document means that it remains a section "Entitled XYZ" according to this definition.

The Document may include Warranty Disclaimers next to the notice which states that this License applies to the Document. These Warranty Disclaimers are considered to be included by reference in this License, but only as regards disclaiming warranties: any other implication that these Warranty Disclaimers may have is void and has no effect on the meaning of this License.

VERBATIM COPYING

You may copy and distribute the Document in any medium, either commercially or noncommercially, provided that this License, the copyright notices, and the license notice saying this License applies to the Document are reproduced in all copies, and that you add no other conditions whatsoever to those of this License. You may not use technical measures to obstruct or control the reading or further copying of the copies you make or distribute. However, you may accept compensation in exchange for copies. If you distribute a large enough number of copies you must also follow the conditions in section 3.

You may also lend copies, under the same conditions stated above, and you may publicly display copies.

COPYING IN QUANTITY

If you publish printed copies (or copies in media that commonly have printed covers) of the Document, numbering more than 100, and the Document's license notice requires Cover Texts, you must enclose the copies in covers that carry, clearly and legibly, all these Cover Texts: Front-Cover Texts on the front cover, and Back-Cover Texts on the back cover. Both covers must also clearly and legibly identify you as the publisher of these copies. The front cover must present the full title with all words of the title equally prominent and visible. You may add other material on the covers in addition. Copying with changes limited to the covers, as long as they preserve the title of the Document and satisfy these conditions, can be treated as verbatim copying in other respects.

If the required texts for either cover are too voluminous to fit legibly, you should put the first ones listed (as many as fit reasonably) on the actual cover, and continue the rest onto adjacent pages.

If you publish or distribute Opaque copies of the Document numbering more than 100, you must either include a machine-readable Transparent copy along with each Opaque copy, or state in or with each Opaque copy a computer-network location from which the general network-using public has access to download using public-standard network protocols a complete Transparent copy of the Document, free of added material. If you use the latter option, you must take reasonably prudent steps, when you begin distribution of Opaque copies in quantity, to ensure that this Transparent copy will remain thus accessible at the stated location until at least one year after the last time you distribute an Opaque copy (directly or through your agents or retailers) of that edition to the public.

It is requested, but not required, that you contact the authors of the Document well before redistributing any large number of copies, to give them a chance to provide you with an updated version of the Document.

MODIFICATIONS

You may copy and distribute a Modified Version of the Document under the conditions of sections 2 and 3 above, provided that you release the Modified Version under precisely this License, with the Modified Version filling the role of the Document, thus licensing distribution and modification of the Modified Version to whoever possesses a copy of it. In addition, you must do these things in the Modified Version:

A. Use in the Title Page (and on the covers, if any) a title distinct from that of the Document, and from those of previous versions (which should, if there were any, be listed in the History section of the Document). You may use the same title as a previous version if the original publisher of that version gives permission.

B. List on the Title Page, as authors, one or more persons or entities responsible for authorship of the modifications in the Modified Version, together with at least five of the principal authors of the Document (all of its principal authors, if it has fewer than five), unless they release you from this requirement.

C. State on the Title page the name of the publisher of the Modified Version, as the publisher.

D. Preserve all the copyright notices of the Document.

E. Add an appropriate copyright notice for your modifications adjacent to the other copyright notices.

F. Include, immediately after the copyright notices, a license notice giving the public permission to use the Modified Version under the terms of this License, in the form shown in the Addendum below.

G. Preserve in that license notice the full lists of Invariant Sections and required Cover Texts given in the Document's license notice.

H. Include an unaltered copy of this License.

I. Preserve the section Entitled "History", Preserve its Title, and add to it an item stating at least the title, year, new authors, and publisher of the Modified Version as given on the Title Page. If there is no section Entitled "History" in the Document, create one stating the title, year, authors, and publisher of the Document as given on its Title Page, then add an item describing the Modified Version as stated in the previous sentence.

J. Preserve the network location, if any, given in the Document for public access to a Transparent copy of the Document, and likewise the network locations given in the Document for previous versions it was based on. These may be placed in the "History" section. You may omit a network location for a work that was published at least four years before the Document itself, or if the original publisher of the version it refers to gives permission.

Beyond the Bleep

K. For any section Entitled "Acknowledgements" or "Dedications", Preserve the Title of the section, and preserve in the section all the substance and tone of each of the contributor acknowledgements and/or dedications given therein.

L. Preserve all the Invariant Sections of the Document, unaltered in their text and in their titles. Section numbers or the equivalent are not considered part of the section titles.

M. Delete any section Entitled "Endorsements". Such a section may not be included in the Modified Version.

N. Do not retitle any existing section to be Entitled "Endorsements" or to conflict in title with any Invariant Section.

O. Preserve any Warranty Disclaimers.

If the Modified Version includes new front-matter sections or appendices that qualify as Secondary Sections and contain no material copied from the Document, you may at your option designate some or all of these sections as invariant. To do this, add their titles to the list of Invariant Sections in the Modified Version's license notice. These titles must be distinct from any other section titles.

You may add a section Entitled "Endorsements", provided it contains nothing but endorsements of your Modified Version by various parties--for example, statements of peer review or that the text has been approved by an organization as the authoritative definition of a standard.

You may add a passage of up to five words as a Front-Cover Text, and a passage of up to 25 words as a Back-Cover Text, to the end of the list of Cover Texts in the Modified Version. Only one passage of Front-Cover Text and one of Back-Cover Text may be added by (or through arrangements made by) any one entity. If the Document already includes a cover text for the same cover, previously added by you or by arrangement made by the same entity you are acting on behalf of, you may not add another; but you may replace the old one, on explicit permission from the previous publisher that added the old one.

The author(s) and publisher(s) of the Document do not by this License give permission to use their names for publicity for or to assert or imply endorsement of any Modified Version.

COMBINING DOCUMENTS

You may combine the Document with other documents released under this License, under the terms defined in section 4 above for modified versions, provided that you include in the combination all of the Invariant Sections of all of the original documents, unmodified, and list them all as Invariant Sections of your combined work in its license notice, and that you preserve all their Warranty Disclaimers.

The combined work need only contain one copy of this License, and multiple identical Invariant Sections may be replaced with a single copy. If there are multiple Invariant Sections with the same name but different contents, make the title of each such section unique by adding at the end of it, in parentheses, the name of the original author or publisher of that section if known, or else a unique number. Make the same adjustment to the section titles in the list of Invariant Sections in the license notice of the combined work.

In the combination, you must combine any sections Entitled "History" in the various original documents, forming one section Entitled "History"; likewise combine any sections Entitled "Acknowledgements", and any sections Entitled "Dedications". You must delete all sections Entitled "Endorsements."

COLLECTIONS OF DOCUMENTS

You may make a collection consisting of the Document and other documents released under this License, and replace the individual copies of this License in the various documents with a single copy that is included in the collection, provided that you follow the rules of this License for verbatim copying of each of the documents in all other respects.

You may extract a single document from such a collection, and distribute it individually under this License, provided you insert a copy of this License into the extracted document, and follow this License in all other respects regarding verbatim copying of that document.

AGGREGATION WITH INDEPENDENT WORKS

A compilation of the Document or its derivatives with other separate and independent documents or works, in or on a volume of a storage or distribution medium, is called an "aggregate" if the copyright resulting from the compilation is not used to limit the legal rights of the compilation's users beyond what the individual works permit. When the Document is included in an aggregate, this License does not apply to the other works in the aggregate which are not themselves derivative works of the Document.

If the Cover Text requirement of section 3 is applicable to these copies of the Document, then if the Document is less than one half of the entire aggregate, the Document's Cover Texts may be placed on covers that bracket the Document within the aggregate, or the electronic equivalent of covers if the Document is in electronic form. Otherwise they must appear on printed covers that bracket the whole aggregate.

TRANSLATION

Translation is considered a kind of modification, so you may distribute translations of the Document under the terms of section 4. Replacing Invariant Sections with translations requires special permission from their copyright holders, but you may include translations of some or all Invariant Sections in addition to the original versions of these Invariant Sections. You may include a translation of this License, and all the license notices in the Document, and any Warranty Disclaimers, provided that you also include the original English version of this License and the original versions of those notices and disclaimers. In case of a disagreement between the translation and the original version of this License or a notice or disclaimer, the original version will prevail.

If a section in the Document is Entitled "Acknowledgements", "Dedications", or "History", the requirement (section 4) to Preserve its Title (section 1) will typically require changing the actual title.

TERMINATION

You may not copy, modify, sublicense, or distribute the Document except as expressly provided for under this License. Any other attempt to copy, modify, sublicense or distribute the Document is void, and will automatically terminate your rights under this License. However, parties who have received copies, or rights, from you under this License will not have their licenses terminated so long as such parties remain in full compliance.

FUTURE REVISIONS OF THIS LICENSE

The Free Software Foundation may publish new, revised versions of the GNU Free Documentation License from time to time. Such new versions will be similar in spirit to the present version, but may differ in detail to address new problems or concerns. See http://www.gnu.org/copyleft/.

Each version of the License is given a distinguishing version number. If the Document specifies that a particular numbered version of this License "or any later version" applies to it, you have the option of following the terms and conditions either of that specified version or of any later version that has been published (not as a draft) by the Free Software Foundation. If the Document does not specify a version number of this License, you may choose any version ever published (not as a draft) by the Free Software Foundation.

Beyond the Bleep

ENDNOTES

CHAPTER 1
THE *WHAT THE BLEEP* PHENOMENON

[1] Gorenfeld, J. March 16, 2005. "What the Bleep Do I Know?" *Orkut Media.* http://media.orkut.com/articles/r0137.html

[2] Hinsdale, J. May 27, 2005 "Einstein in the West, Quanta in the East," *PBS.org* http://www.pbs.org/wnet/religionandethics/week839/exclusive.html

[3] Columbia University mathematics professor, Peter Woit's blog: http://www.math.columbia.edu/~woit/blog/archives/000083.html

[4] IMDB blog: http://www.imdb.com/title/tt0399877/board/nest/11662694

[5] Miller, D.I. April 4, 2004. "Fred Alan Wolf from 'What the Bleep Do We Know?' On Spirituality," *SFGate.com* http://sfgate.com/cgi-bin/article.cgi?file=/g/a/2005/04/04/findrelig.DTL

[6] Yahr, H. September 9, 2004. "Let's Get Metaphysical," *Salon.com*

[7] Grove, M. March 17, 2004. "Gibson Breaks Hollywood's Ten Commands," *HollywoodReporter.com* http://www.hollywoodreporter.com/thr/columns/grove_display.jsp?vnu_content_id=1000464071

[8] Ibid.

[9] Ibid.

[10] *What The Bleep* webpage: http://www.whatthebleep.com/streetteams/

[11] Hettrick, S. April 25, 2005. "'Bleep' Has Deep Support," *Variety.com* http://www.variety.com/article/VR1117921605?categoryid=20&cs=1

[12] *What The Bleep* webpage: http://www.whatthebleep.com/cal/

[13] http://www.thequantumcruise.com/

[14] Bageant, J. February 2004. "Poor, White and Pissed: A Guide to the White Trash Planet for Urban Liberals"

CHAPTER 2
HOW DOES REALITY WORK?

[1] Goswami, A. Ph.D., quoted from the film, *What The Bleep Do We Know?!*

[2] This 'mini-solar system' concept is now out of date but it still

helps to illustrate the atom in the simplest way. As Jeff Satinover says, "Electrons don't really have discrete orbits (i.e., trajectories). They act like delocalized waves…that occupy "orbitals" – fuzzy configurations of probability amplitudes…" Satinover, J. 2001. *The Quantum Brain*. (Wiley & Sons, New York) p. 180

[3] Wikipedia The Free Encyclopedia:
http://en.wikipedia.org/wiki/Many-worlds_interpretation

[4] Satinover, J. M.D., quoted from the film, *What The Bleep Do We Know?!*

[5] *What The Bleep* Newsletter: May 13, 2005.
The Bleeping Herald Vol. 1, No. 1
http://www.whatthebleep.com/herald/issue1-quandaries.shtml

[6] Fred Alan Wolf website: http://www.fredalanwolf.com/page5.htm

[7] Dawkins, R. May 16, 2005 "The Minds Boggle," *The Guardian*

[8] British Channel 4 website: http://www.channel4.com/film/reviews/film.jsp?id=144354

[9] Migueijo, J. May 16, 2005 "The Minds Boggle," *The Guardian*

[10] Margolis, J. May 18, 2005 *The Independent Online Edition*.
http://enjoyment.independent.co.uk/film/news/story.jsp?story=639340

[11] Mone, G. "Cult Science," *Popular Science*, October 2004 http://www.popsci.com/popsci/science/article/0,20967,699379,00.html

[12] Satinover, J. quoted from the film, *What The Bleep Do We Know?!*

[13] Goswami, A. quoted from the film, *What The Bleep Do We Know?!*

[14] Shermer, M. January 2005. "Quantum Quackery," *Scientific American*.

[15] Stuart Hameroff's website: http://www.quantumconsciousness.org/hackery.htm

[16] Goswami, A. Undated. Interview by Craig Hamilton for *What is Enlightenment Magazine* http://www.wie.org/j20/goswami.asp?page=2

[17] Amit Goswami, Ph.D. 1993. *The Self-Aware Universe*, (Penguin Putnam Inc.) p. 10

[18] Ibid.

CHAPTER 3
DAVID ALBERT, PH.D. & HOW REALITY DOES NOT WORK

[1] "I am Ramtha, 'the Ram'. In the ancient language of my times, it means 'the god'. I am the great Ram of the Hindu people, for

I was the first man born of the womb of woman and the loins of man who ever ascended from this plane." Knight, J.Z. 1999 *Ramtha: The White Book* (JZK Publishing, Inc.) p. 27

[2] Gorenfeld, J. September 16, 2004. "'Bleep' of faith" *Salon.com*. (Emphasis added). http://www.salon.com/ent/feature/2004/09/16/bleep/index1.html

[3] Lydgate, C. December 22, 2004 "What the #$*! is Ramtha" *Willamette Week*

[4] Mone, G. October 2004. "Cult Science" *Popular Science.com*. (Emphasis added). http://www.popsci.com/popsci/science/article/0,20967,699379,00.html

[5] Gorenfeld, J. September 16, 2004. "'Bleep' of faith" *Salon.com*. (Emphasis added). http://www.salon.com/ent/feature/2004/09/16/bleep/index1.html

[6] Albert, David. Z. 1992. *Quantum Mechanics and Experience* (Harvard University Press).

[7] Albert, D. February 2005. *The Central Puzzle of Quantum Mechanics* Audio CD (Axiom Prophet's Conference). (Emphases added).

[8] Ibid.

[9] Trull, D. 1997 "Toilet Paper Plagiarism." *ParaScope.com* (Emphasis added). http://www.parascope.com/articles/slips/fs_151.htm

[10] Albert, D.Z. 1983 "On Quantum-Mechanical Automata." *Physics Letters*. Vol. 98A pp. 249-252 (Emphasis added).

[11] Wolf, F.A. "The Quantum Mechanics of Dreams and the Emergence of Self-Awareness." 1996. *Toward a Scientific Basis for Consciousness*, Eds. S. R. Hameroff, A. W. Kaszniak, and A. C. Scott. (The MIT Press) pp. 451-67.

CHAPTER 4
JEFFREY SATINOVER, M.D. & THE QUANTUM BRAIN

[1] See Satinover's bio on his website: http://www.satinover.com/main.htm

[2] Ibid.

[3] http://www.outfront.org/library/fact.html

[4] Gorenfeld, J. September 16, 2004. "'Bleep' of Faith." *Salon.com*

[5] Singel, R. November 19, 2004. "Internet Porn: Worse Than Crack?" *Wired.com*
http://www.wired.com/news/technology/0,1282,65772,00.html?tw=wn_tophead_4

[6] Satinover, J. 2001. *The Quantum Brain.* (Wiley & Sons) p. 80

[7] Op. Cit. p.87

[8] Op. Cit. p.98

[9] Dawkins, R. 1995. *River Out of Eden: A Darwinian View of Life* (Basic Books). p. 133

[10] Satinover, J. 2001. *The Quantum Brain.* (Wiley & Sons). p.115

[11] Op. Cit. p. 174

[12] Op. Cit. p. 192 (Emphasis added).

[13] Stuchebrukhov, A.A. 1996 "Tunneling Currents in Electron Transfer in Proteins. II. Calculation of Electronic Superexchange Matrix Element and Tunneling Currents Using Non-orthogonal Basis Sets," *Journal of Chemical Physics* #105 pp. 10819-10829

[14] Satinover, J. 2001. *The Quantum Brain.* (Wiley & Sons) p. 1810

[15] Op. Cit p. 188

[16] Op. Cit p. 210

[17] Op. Cit p. 214

[18] Op. Cit p. 217

CHAPTER 5
STUART HAMEROFF, M.D. &
ORCHESTRATED OBJECTIVE REDUCTION

[1] Stuart Hameroff's website: http://www.quantumconsciousness. org/interests.html

[2] Penrose, R. 2005. "The Theory of everything," *Nature Magazine* #433, pp. 257–259

[3] Hameroff, S.R. 2005. Letter to *Scientific American* magazine in response to article by Michael Shermer, "Quantum Quackery". http://www.quantumconsciousness.org/hackery.htm

[4] Penrose, R. & Hameroff, S.R. 1996. "Orchestrated Objective Reduction of Quantum Coherence in Brain Microtubules: The "Orch OR" Model for Consciousness" *Toward a Science of Consciousness - The First Tucson Discussions and Debates*, eds. Hameroff, S.R., Kaszniak, A.W. and Scott, A.C. (MIT Press) pp. 507-540

[5] Ibid.

[6] Penrose, R. 1996. *Shadows of the Mind* (Oxford University Press).

[7] Shermer, M. January 2005. "Quantum Hackery" *Scientific American* magazine.

[8] Hameroff, S.R. 2005. Letter to *Scientific American* magazine in response to article by Michael Shermer, "Quantum Quackery". (Emphasis added). http://www.quantumconsciousness.org/hackery.htm

[9] Satinover, J. 2001. *The Quantum Brain*. (Wiley & Sons) p. 230

[10] Hameroff, S.R. 2005. Letter to *Scientific American* magazine in response to article by Michael Shermer, "Quantum Quackery". http://www.quantumconsciousness.org/hackery.htm (Emphases added).

[11] Hameroff quoted in interview submitted by Greg Jan. 21, 2005. *DailyGrail.com* "The Quantum Mind of Stuart Hameroff" http://www.dailygrail.com/node/842

[12] Hameroff quoted in interview submitted by Greg Jan. 21, 2005. *DailyGrail.com* "The Quantum Mind of Stuart Hameroff" http://www.dailygrail.com/node/842

[13] Overbye, D. Nov. 9, 2002 "Are They a) Geniuses or b) Jokers? French Physicists' Cosmic Theory Creates a Big Bang of Its Own" *The New York Times*

[14] Penrose, R. 2005. "The Theory of everything," *Nature Magazine* #433, pp. 257–259

CHAPTER 6.
FRED ALAN WOLF, PH.D. & THE YOGA OF TIME TRAVEL

[1] Margolis, J. May 18, 2005. "The Meaning of Life (or a Load of Old Quantum?)" *The Independent Online Edition*. (Emphases added). http://enjoyment.independent.co.uk/film/news/story.jsp?story=639340

[2] Egeln, H. September 12, 2004. "*What The Bleep's*" Director Arntz Talks With Movie Theater Audience." *Wonderland Chronicles* http://community2.webtv.net/@HH!8C!1F!5146F5105C50/AOKSpacer/PROJECTWONDERLAND/page8.html

[3] Wolf, F.A. 2004. *The Yoga of Time Travel: How the Mind Can Defeat Time*. (Quest Books) pp. 13-14

[4] Iyengar, B.K.S. 1996. *Light on the Yoga Sutras of Patanjali* (Thorsons) p. 33

[5] Wolf, F.A. 2004. *The Yoga of Time Travel: How the Mind Can Defeat Time*. (Quest Books) p. 59. (Emphasis added).

[6] Kolers, P. & von Grünau, M. 1976. "Shape and Color in Apparent Motion," *Vision Research* Vol. 16 pp. 329-35.

[7] Wolf, F.A. 2004. *The Yoga of Time Travel: How the Mind Can Defeat Time*. (Quest Books) pp. 64-67.

[8] Cramer, J.G. 1980. "Generalized Absorber Theory and the Einstein-Podolsky-Rosen Paradox," *Physical Review* D22:362. Also see Cramer 1986, "The Transactional Interpretation of Quantum Mechanics," *Reviews of Modern Physics* 58, no. 3 (July).

[9] Wolf, F.A. 2004. *The Yoga of Time Travel: How the Mind Can Defeat Time.* (Quest Books) pp. 154-156.

[10] Op Cit. pp. 157.

[11] Open System For Geniuses Blog: http://opensys.blogsome.com/

[12] My secret physicist advisor's other blog: http://opensys.blogspot.com/

[13] Fred Alan Wolf website: http://www.fredalanwolf.com/page5.htm

[14] Oldstein, S. 1997. "Spontaneous Localization" Rutgers University Mathematics Dept. website:
http://www.math.rutgers.edu/~oldstein/papers/qts/node3.html

[15] *Are There Quantum Jumps?* Conference website: http://www.ts.infn.it/events/QM2005/

[16] http://www.opensys.blogspot.com and http://www.opensys.blogsome.com

[17] Wolf, F.A. 2004. *The Yoga of Time Travel: How the Mind Can Defeat Time.* (Quest Books) p. 197.

[18] Op Cit. pp. 209.

[19] Op Cit. p. 115.

[20] Op Cit. p. 125.

[21] Op Cit. p. 127.

CHAPTER 7.
AMIT GOSWAMI, PH.D. & MONISTIC IDEALISM

[1] Shermer, M. 2005 "Quantum Quackery," *Scientific American* 292(1):234 2005

[2] Amit Goswami, 2004 quoted from the film, *What The Bleep Do We Know?!*

[3] Goswami, A. 1993, *The Self-Aware Universe*, (Penguin Putnam Inc.) p. 9

[4] Op. Cit. p.17

[5] Ibid. (Emphasis added).

[6] Op. Cit. p. 84

[7] Op. Cit. p. 47 (Emphasis added).

[8] Op. Cit. p. 48

[9] Op. Cit. p. 167

[10] Op. Cit. p. 190

[11] Op. Cit. p. 192

[12] Wolf, F.A. 1982. *Taking the Quantum Leap.* San Francisco: Harper and Row

[13] Goswami, A. *The Self-Aware Universe*, 1993 Penguin Putnam Inc., New York. p. 140

[14] Op. Cit. p. 141

[15] Op. Cit. p. 205

[16] Op. Cit. p. 215

[17] Op. Cit. p. 263

[18] Wheeler, J.A. 1982. "The Computer and the Universe." *International Journal of Theoretical Physics* 21:557-72

[19] Humphrey, N. and Weiskrantz, L. 1967. "Vision in Monkeys After Removal of the Striate Cortex." *Nature* 215:595-97

[20] Humphrey, N. 1972. "Seeing and Nothingness." *New Scientist* 53.682.

[21] Goswami, A. 1993, *The Self-Aware Universe*, (Penguin Putnam Inc.) p. 64

[22] Puthoff, H.E. & Targ, R. 1976. "A Perceptual Channel for Information Transfer Over Kilometer Distances: Historical Perspective and Recent Research." *Proceedings of the IEEE* 64:329-54.

[23] Jahn, R. 1982. "The Persistent Paradox of Psychic Phenomena: An Engineering Perspective." *Proceedings of the IEEE* 70:135-70.

[24] Goswami, A. 1993, *The Self-Aware Universe*, (Penguin Putnam Inc.) p. 131 (Emphasis added).

[25] Op. Cit. p. 63 (Emphasis added).

CHAPTER 8.
YCYOR: DO YOU CREATE YOUR OWN REALITY?

[1] Lydgate, C. December 22, 2004. "What the #$*! is Ramtha," *Willamette Week*.

[2] Yahr, H. September 9, 2004. "Let's Get Metaphysical," *Salon.com*

[3] Roberts, J. 1974, 1994 *The Nature of Personal Reality* Amber-Allen Publishing pp. 10-440

[4] Lydgate, C. December 22, 2004. "What the #$*! is Ramtha," *Willamette Week*.

[5] Greene, B. April 8, 2005. "One Hundred Years of Uncertainty," *New York Times*.

[6] Wolf, F.A. 2004. *The Yoga of Time Travel: How the Mind Can Defeat Time* (Quest Books) p. 116

[7] Blanchard, Ph. & Jadczyck, A. 1998 "Time and Events," *International Journal of Theoretical Physics* pp. 227-233. http://arxiv.org/abs/quant-ph/9702018

[8] Jadczyk, A. April 2005. "Simultaneous Measurement of Non-Commuting Observables and Quantum Fractals on Complex Projective Spaces," *Chinese Journal of Physics* http://psroc.phys.ntu.

edu.tw/cjp/find_content.php?year=2005&vol=43&no=2

[9] Lydgate, C. December 22, 2004. "What the #$*! is Ramtha," *Willamette Week*

[10] Wilber, K. 2002. *Boomeritis: A Novel That Will Set You Free!* (Shambhala) pp. 36-389 (Emphases added).

[11] Princeton Engineering Anomalies Research Scientific Study of Consciousness-Related Physical Phenomena website: http://www.princeton.edu/~pear/3.html

[12] Jahn, R. G., Dunne, B. J., Nelson, R. D., Dobyns, Y. H. & Bradish, G. J. 1997. "Correlations of Random Binary Sequences with Pre-Stated Operator Intention: A Review of a 12-Year Program". *Journal of Scientific Exploration*, Vol. 11, No. 3, pp. 345–367

[13] Wolf, F.A. 2004. *The Yoga of Time Travel: How the Mind Can Defeat Time* (Quest Books) pp. 169-170

[14] Goswami, A. 1993, *The Self-Aware Universe*, (Penguin Putnam Inc.) p. 187 (Emphasis in original).

[15] Op. Cit. p. 97 (Emphasis added).

[16] Wilber, K. 2002. *Boomeritis: A Novel That Will Set You Free!* (Shambhala) pp. 328-338

[17] Gurevitch, A. May 19, 2004. "Interview: Will Arntz: Down the Rabbit Hole" *dtheatre.com*
http://www.whatthebleep.com/reviews/dtheatre.htm

[18] Peak Oil websites: http://www.peakoil.org/ and http://www.fromthewilderness.com/

[19] Mieszkowski, K. May 14, 2005. "After the Oil is Gone" *Salon.com*
http://www.salon.com/news/feature/2005/05/14/kunstler/index_np.html

CHAPTER 9.
MASARU EMOTO & THE HIDDEN MESSAGES IN WATER

[1] Emoto, M. 2004 *The Hidden Messages of Water* (Beyond Words Publishing). p. xxvi

[2] Stevens, J. 1992. *The Art of Peace* (Shambhala)

[3] *What The Bleep* website: http://www.whatthebleep.com/crystals/

[4] Emoto's website: http://www.masaru-emoto.net/english/eprofile.html

[5] Tiller, W.A., Dibble, W.E., Kohane, M.J. 2001 *Conscious Acts of Creation* (Pavior Publishing) p. 70.

[6] McTaggart, L. 2002. *The Field: The Quest for the Secret Force of the Universe.* (HarperCollins) pp. 61-63

[7] Ibid.

[8] Op. Cit. p. 64

[9] DigiBio website: http://www.digibio.com/

[10] Benveniste, J., Jurgens, P et al. 1997. "Transatlantic Transfer of Digitized Antigen Signal by Telephone Link." *Journal of Allergy and Clinical Immunology.* 99:S175

CHAPTER 10.
WILLIAM TILLER & CONSCIOUS ACTS OF CREATION

[1] Tiller, W.A., Dibble, W.E., Kohane, M.J. 2001 *Conscious Acts of Creation* (Pavior Publishing) p. xi (Emphasis in original).

[2] Ibid. (Emphasis in original).

[3] Op. Cit. p. 1

[4] Op. Cit p. 29

[5] William Tiller's website: http://www.tiller.org/

[6] Tiller, W.A., Dibble, W.E., Kohane, M.J. 2001 *Conscious Acts of Creation* (Pavior Publishing) p. 378

[7] Tiller, W.A. January 2003. "Conscious Acts of Creation: The Emergence of a New Physics" *The International Journal of Healing & Caring, Online* 3 (1). P. 8

[8] http://www.opensys.blogspot.com

CHAPTER 11.
JOHN HAGELIN, PH.D. FOR PRESIDENT

[1] Hagelin's website: http://www.hagelin.org

[2] World Peace Endowment website, one of numerous sites produced by the TM™ movement: http://www.worldpeaceendowment.org/invincibility/invincibility7.html

[3] Anderson, C. Sept. 10, 1992 Nature, #359

[4] Columbia University mathematics professor, Peter Woit's blog: http://www.math.columbia.edu/~woit/blog/archives/000083.html (Emphases added).

[5] Hagelin's personal website: http://hagelin.org/

[6] Global Country of World Peace website: http://www.globalcountry.org

[7] Cult awareness website: http://www.trancenet.org/

[8] Op. Cit. http://www.trancenet.org/nlp/secrets/meaning.shtml

[9] Op. Cit. http://www.trancenet.org/nlp/secrets/money.shtml and http://www.trancenet.org/nlp/secrets/money.shtml

[10] D'Antonio, M. 1992. *Heaven and Earth: Dispatches From America's*

Spiritual Frontier (Crown Publishing Group) Ch. 6

[11] Midgett, M. & Karasz, A. 2000. "Transcendental Meditation." University of Virginia's Religious Movements webpage: http://religiousmovements.lib.virginia.edu/nrms/tm.html

[12] http://en.wikipedia.org/wiki/What_the_Bleep_Do_We_Know%3F!#Controversial_studies

[13] Institute of Science, Technology and Public Policy website: http://www.istpp.org/crime_prevention/ (Emphasis added).

CHAPTER 12.
CANDACE PERT, PH.D. & THE MOLECULES OF EMOTION

[1] Pert, C. 1997. *Molecules of Emotion: The Science Behind Mind-Body Medicine.* (Simon & Schuster). pp. 23-25 (Emphasis added).

[2] Op. Cit. pp. 61-62

[3] Op. Cit. p. 84

[4] Op. Cit. p. 85

[5] Op. Cit. p. 111

[6] Op. Cit. p. 20

[7] Op. Cit. pp. 99-158 (Emphasis added).

[8] Op. Cit. p. 109

[9] Op. Cit. p. 215 (Emphasis added).

[10] Ruff, M. and Pert, C. September 1984 *Science.*

[11] Pert, C. 1997. *Molecules of Emotion: The Science Behind Mind-Body Medicine.* (Simon & Schuster). pp. 228-229

[12] Op. Cit. p. 207

[13] Op. Cit. p. 217

[14] Op. Cit. p. 218

[15] Op. Cit. p. 231

[16] Op. Cit. pp. 177-178

CHAPTER 13.
JOSEPH DISPENZA, D.C. & NEUROPEPTIDE ADDICTION

[1] Dispenza, J. quoted from *What The Bleep Do We Know!?*

[2] Op. Cit.

CHAPTER 14.
RAMTHA vs. RELIGION

[1] Gorenfeld, J. September 16, 2004. "'Bleep' of Faith" *Salon.com*

[2] Gurevich, A. May 19, 2004 "Interview: Will Arntz: Down the

Rabbit Hole." *Dtheatre.com* (Emphasis added).

[3] Knight, J.Z. October 7-8, 1995. "Beginning C&E™ Workshop," *Ramtha Dialogues*® Tape #324,

[4] University of Virginia's Religious Movements webpage: http://religiousmovements.lib.virginia.edu/nrms/Ramtha.html

[5] Knight, J.Z. 1999 *Ramtha: The White Book* (JZK Publishing, Yelm WA) p. 27

[6] Op. Cit. p. 41

[7] *The Holy Bible*, Book of Daniel Chapter 10, verses 6-9

[8] Statement by J.Z. Knight:
http://www.ramtha.com/html/media/press-rels/97.stm

[9] http://www.whatthebleep.com/guide/

[10] http://en.wikipedia.org/wiki/Edgar_Mitchell

[11] Hill, G. 1998. "The Failure Of The Human Potential Movement: From Self-Actualization To Experientialism." (Emphasis added). http://www.pacificnet.net/~cmoore/ghill/esalen2.htm

[12] Allegedly printed on the back cover of the Ramtha DVD, *Ramtha - Create Your Day: An Invitation to Open Your Mind*, directed by Mark Vicente. Produced by RSE. Release Date: March 16, 2005. (Emphasis added).
http://www.amazon.com/o/ASIN/B0007ZHNBC/103-4270839-4214248?SubscriptionId=1614NPD3XH4PRYYEDS82#product-details

[13] Knight, J.Z. 1999 *Ramtha: The White Book* (JZK Publishing, Yelm WA) pp. 105-106

[14] Gurevich, A. May 19, 2004 "Interview: Will Arntz: Down the Rabbit Hole." *Dtheatre.com*
http://www.whatthebleep.com/reviews/dtheatre.htm

[15] Bennett, R. 2003. (Emphasis added). http://www.christiananswers.net/q-eden/mysticism-bennett.html

[16] Goswami, A. 1993, *The Self-Aware Universe*, (Penguin Putnam Inc.) p. 56

[17] McGarry, P. June 1, 2002. "Bishops Say Ledwith Faced Abuse Claims." *The Irish Times*. http://www.ireland.com/newspaper/front/2002/0601/4164376683HM1LEDFRONT.html

[18] Wilber, K. 2002. *Boomeritis: A Novel That Will Set You Free!* (Shambhala) pp. 334-338 (Emphasis added).

[19] RSE Press Release: http://www.ramtha.com/html/media/press-rels/97.stm

[20] Lydgate, C. December 22, 2004 "What the #$*! is Ramtha". *Willamette Week*

[21] RSE website: http://www.ramtha.com/html/aboutus/faqs/school/cost.stm

[22] Elfin Magical Capes website: http://www.elfinmagicalcapes.com/

[23] Outback Boutique website: http://www.outbackboutique.com/

CONCLUSION

[1] Albert, D. February 2005. *The Central Puzzle of Quantum Mechanics* Audio CD (Axiom Prophet's Conference).

[2] Satinover, J. 2001. *The Quantum Brain.* (Wiley & Sons) p. 5 (Emphasis added).

[3] Hinsdale, J. May 27, 2005 "Einstein in the West, Quanta in the East," PBS.org http://www.pbs.org/wnet/religionandethics/week839/exclusive.html

[4] Satinover, J. 2001. *The Quantum Brain.* (Wiley & Sons) p. 217 (Emphasis added).

[5] What The Bleep webpage: http://www.whatthebleep.com/spiritual/ where the following websites are recommended: http://www.Movingmessagesmedia.com and http://www.Spiritualcinemacircle.com

GLOSSARY

[1] Pert, C. 1997. *Molecules of Emotion: The Science Behind Mind-Body Medicine.* (Simon & Schuster). p. 187

[2] The American Heritage® Dictionary of the English Language: Fourth Edition. 2000.

[3] Ibid.

[4] Pert, C. 1997. *Molecules of Emotion: The Science Behind Mind-Body Medicine.* (Simon & Schuster). p. 350

[5] The American Heritage® Dictionary of the English Language: Fourth Edition. 2000.

[6] Pert, C. 1997. *Molecules of Emotion: The Science Behind Mind-Body Medicine.* (Simon & Schuster). p. 351

[7] Stuart Hameroff's website: http://www.quantumconsciousness.org/penrose-hameroff/orchOR.html

[8] Pert, C. 1997. *Molecules of Emotion: The Science Behind Mind-Body Medicine.* (Simon & Schuster). p. 352

[9] The American Heritage® Dictionary of the English Language:

Fourth Edition. 2000.

[10] Ibid.

[11] Ibid.

[12] Pert, C. 1997. *Molecules of Emotion: The Science Behind Mind-Body Medicine.* (Simon & Schuster). p. 351

INDEX

A

Q

U

V

W

ABOUT THE AUTHOR

Alexandra Bruce's articles on urban legends, metaphysical and quantum physics themes have been published in Paranoia Magazine, Steamshovel Press, Borderland Sciences and Disinfo.com. She recently translated the book *Celestial Secrets, The Hidden History of the Mystery of Fátima* with a Foreword by Jim Marrs. She lives in Rio de Janeiro and Southampton, New York.